SPECIAL EDITION
2005

By Mary Packard
and the Editors of Ripley Entertainment Inc.

SCHOLASTIC INC.

New York   Toronto   London   Auckland   Sydney

Mexico City   New Delhi   Hong Kong   Buenos Aires

Library of Congress Cataloging-in-Publication Data available

Library of Congress Cataloging-in-Publication Data
Packard, Mary.
   Ripley's believe it or not! / by Mary Packard and the editors of Ripley
Entertainment, Inc.—Special ed., 2005
      p. cm.
Includes index.
ISBN 0-439-65191-3
1. Curiosities and wonders—Juvenile literature. I. Title: Believe it or not!.
II. Ripley Entertainment, Inc. III. Title. AG243.P24 2004
031.02—dc22

2004042885

Developed by Nancy Hall, Inc.

Edited by Linda Falken

Designed by Atif Toor

Cover design by Louise Bova

Photo research by Laura Miller, Zan Carter, and Sharon Lennon

12 11 10 9 8 7 6 5 4 3 2 1   4 5 6 7 8 9/0

Printed in China

First printing, September 2004

CONTENTS

RIPLEY's WILD WORLD

For decades, Ripley's Believe It or Not! has been one of the most popular entertainment features in the world. More than 80 million people around the globe have been shocked and astonished by Robert Ripley's collection of bizarre facts. Are you ready to join them? Inside these pages, you'll find fascinating facts, amazing acts, and bizarre behavior, all based on the files of Robert Ripley. Though they seem too strange to be true, each and every one is genuine. After all, sometimes "there's nothing stranger than the truth."

Believe It!

In 1842, P. T. Barnum exhibited a creation he called "The Feejee Mermaid"—and many people believed it was real!

At mealtime, Tessa the cat prefers to eat with a fork, a spoon—or even a pair of chopsticks!

Jo Jo the Dog-Faced Boy suffered from a condition called "werewolf syndrome"—he had hair growing uncontrollably all over his face!

Ripley ON THE GO

The Birth of the BION

A man with an eye for the odd, Robert Ripley lived quite an unusual life himself. His amazing career began when he created a new kind of sports comic strip featuring exceptional athletic feats, from a man who walked backward across North America to the fastest recorded three-legged race. Though it was a last-minute idea, the strip was a huge hit! Ripley's publisher, editor, and readers begged for more wacky facts—and Ripley's Believe It or Not! was born.

Early Start

By age 14, Robert Ripley had already sold a drawing to a popular magazine!

In Search of the Unusual

Ripley traveled a distance equal to 18 complete trips around the globe in his quest for unusual facts! From Europe to South America, Asia to Alaska, Ripley discovered curious customs, peculiar people, and strange events. He also received more than a million letters per year from people sharing weird facts of their own. Everything was recorded in the "Ripley Files," which are still used today as resources for the Believe It or Not! television show, videos, museums—and this book!

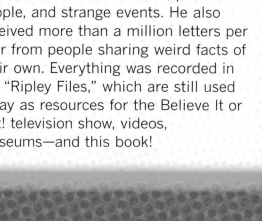

At one time, Ripley's cartoons appeared daily in over 300 newspapers in 42 countries!

Ripley Entertainment

The popularity of Ripley's cartoons led to syndication, and within a few years, he became the first millionaire cartoonist in the world. Ripley made film shorts, published best-selling books full of amazing facts and photos, hosted his own radio hour, and created his own television show.

Ripley's Odditorium in Gatlinburg, Tennessee

RIPLEY FILES:

Throughout this book, you'll find cartoons from the Ripley archives. The date that each cartoon was published is shown at the top.

See It to Believe It!

Ripley's first Odditorium, a museum of the bizarre, opened at the 1933 Century of Progress World's Fair in Chicago. It was one of the most popular attractions and led to many more Odditoriums. Today, there are 27 in operation around the world.

PECULIAR PAGES!

Turn the page for awesome attractions, ridiculous rescues, creepy critters, and much, *much* more!

7

1

GOING GLOBAL

WACKY PLANET

The Pits

When people living in Battle Mountain, Nevada, learned that their town was voted the "Armpit of the Nation" by *The Washington Post* newspaper, they decided not to make a big stink about it. Instead, with the sponsorship of Proctor & Gamble, the company that makes Old Spice products, they hosted the Old Spice Festival of the Pit. The celebration featured such attractions as the deodorant toss, the sweaty T-shirt contest, and the armpit beauty pageant. A stinky time was had by all.

Pests for Pets

Some animal lovers in Australia keep cockroaches as pets, but they're not just ordinary cockroaches. They're wingless Australian burrowing cockroaches—and they're as big as the palm of your hand! The advantages of having one of these monsters for a pet? They don't fetch or roll over, but on the other hand, they don't bite, they're not fussy eaters, and they don't need to be taken for a walk in the rain at five o'clock in the morning.

SCENT-SATIONAL

A tribal custom in New Guinea takes some of the stink out of saying good-bye. Close friends and relatives stick their fingers in each other's armpits and rub the scent on themselves so that they'll have a fragrant reminder of their loved ones after parting.

Hip, Hip, Splat!

It is the custom in Brasov, Romania, for wedding guests to throw the groom into the air three times, but they're supposed to catch him three times as well. When a tossing attempt at one wedding ended in failure, the bridegroom suffered head and chest injuries and ended up spending his honeymoon in the hospital.

Leash Law

It's against the law to walk a pet snake on a leash through a public park in Osnago, Italy. Snake walking had become a popular trend there until the town's mayor decided that the fad was too dangerous.

RIPLEY FILE: 12.10.70

Birdman! Author Alexandre Dumas (1824–1895) had a pet vulture that he walked on a leash through the streets of Paris, France.

GLOBAL WARMING

Love Rules

The streets are packed, the techno music is loud, and the people are "stylin'" in their most outrageous outfits. More than 500,000 music fans gathered in Berlin for the 2003 Loveparade. It all started in 1989, shortly before the fall of the Berlin Wall, with a DJ called Dr. Motte, who led about 150 people in a musical demonstration for "peace, tolerance, respect, and understanding between nations." Since then, the parade has become an annual event for lovers of electronic dance music from all around the globe.

GREETINGS!

In December 1989, James Lawlor of Fairfield, Iowa, sent an 800-foot-long Happy New Year card signed by 500,000 Americans to then Soviet President Mikhail Gorbachev!

Major Lip Lock

Hoping to attract tourists from all over the world, the Italian town of Riccione hosted a series of kissing contests in July 2003. The contests were held on land, underwater, and even on a basketball court to see which couple could sink the most basketballs while joined at the lip!

Sew Big!

Imagine creating such a massive needlepoint tapestry that it would need to be displayed in a space the size of an airplane hangar! It took 600 volunteers from five countries to create the three-story tapestry that spells out the word "welcome" in 102 languages. The finished work was displayed on July 3, 2002, at the World Youth Day events in Downsview Park, Canada.

Petal Perfect!

The Feast of Corpus Christi is celebrated each year in Genzano, Italy, with a communion procession down a street carpeted with 13 religious pictures—all made with flower petals. Townspeople spend two weeks collecting flowers. The petals are pulled off, sorted by color, and kept in a cool place. Before dawn on the feast day, the picture designs are drawn in chalk. The townspeople then fill in the designs with petals. Amazingly, the 1,017-foot-long carpet of intricate floral pictures is completed in just a few hours.

AROUND THE WORLD

Terminal Madness

Traveling on Canadian airlines during the Christmas holidays just got safer. That's because fruitcakes are no longer welcome on that country's airplanes. It seems the traditional confections are too dense to be identified by the X-ray scanners—and who knows what might be lurking inside!

Feeling Sheepish

The next time you visit a famous landmark, keep an eye out for an unusual fellow sightseer—in the form of a miniature hand-painted plaster sheep. Created by San Francisco artist James Hartman, the sheep may be found at just about any famous tourist attraction, from the Eiffel Tower to the Lincoln Memorial in Washington, D.C. It all started when Hartman's family and friends took the sheep on their travels, snapped their pictures, and sent the photos back to Hartman. Unlike their human shepherds, the sheep never came home. To date, about 2,000 sheep have traveled the globe. Now, Hartman says, "We'd like to get a sheep on the moon."

ICEBOX

There is an ice hall in the Swiss Alps that contains a stove, table, and piano—all carved from the ice of a glacier.

Way Down Under

One of the most bizarre caves in the world, the Cave of the Swallows is about a five-hour drive from Mexico City, Mexico. It is named for the swallows—at least 100,000—that live inside it.

The cave is deep enough to hold the Empire State Building, which is 102 stories tall! It's possible to rappel to the bottom even though the walls are overhung, but daredevils like Jim Surber prefer to parachute down. Risking life and limb, they free-fall for several seconds at speeds of up to 100 miles per hour. Even after the free fall ends, drifting too close to the jagged walls could shred the parachute or it could collapse should any of the birds get tangled in the lines.

Most of the cave's explorers, however, say the journey is well worth the risks. The landscape at the bottom is like nothing they've ever seen. No direct sunlight reaches the ground there, but glossy emerald-green moss covers the cave's floors and walls. When it's time to return, visitors are hauled up by a winch, two at a time.

WACKY WONDERS

Endless Summer

At Japan's Ocean Dome, visitors can enjoy the world's largest indoor beach, complete with nonstick artificial sand, plastic palm trees, and an "ocean" of salt-free water for swimming and surfing. About the size of three football fields, the Ocean Dome guarantees visitors perfect weather every day of the year, with never a jellyfish sting or a sunburn to spoil the fun.

Pipe Dream

Covering 3.5 acres, the Great Stalacpipe Organ in the Luray Caverns of Virginia is the largest musical instrument in the world. Built in 1954, the organ uses natural stalactites instead of metal pipes to make music. Its creator, Leland Sprinkle, a mathematician and scientist, deliberately chose stalactites that would perfectly match the musical scale.

RIPLEY FILE: 7.28.63

Tears for years! On Mount Sipylos near Manisa, Turkey, is a rock formation that looks like a woman's profile. In 800 B.C.E., the Greek poet Homer referred to it as Niobe in his epic poem *The Iliad*. Niobe was a goddess who was turned to stone by the god Zeus. Water seeping through the rock has made "Niobe" appear to be weeping for more than 2,800 years!

PEEKABOO!

In 1996, Henrik Lehmann and Malene Botoft spent several weeks in a 320-square-foot Plexiglas habitat, complete with books, TV, and computer—in a zoo in Denmark!

Making a Splash

In Valencia, Spain, L'Oceanogràfic, Europe's largest aquarium, is almost entirely underwater! More than 9 million gallons of water—enough to fill 12 Olympic-size swimming pools—fill its underground tanks. Visitors enter through buildings that rise from a lake, then pass through crystal-clear tunnels to view the 45,000 fish in various marine habitats, watch a laser light show, and dine in a submarine restaurant—watched by the fish, of course.

Earth, Sweat, and Years

The Great Wall of China averages about 33 feet in height and is wide enough for ten people to walk along side by side. Spanning 4,500 miles of mountainous terrain in northern China, it is large enough to make an 8-foot-high, 3-foot-thick belt to wrap around Earth's middle. Constructed entirely by hand out of earth, stone, and bricks, it took workers hundreds of years to build. Many laborers died during its construction, and some are buried in the wall itself.

WORDPLAY

What a Croc!

Crocodiles have glands that secrete moisture to wet their eyes when they've been out of the water for a while. Since the glands are near the throat muscles, moisture may be forced out when the crocodile is devouring prey. Does the croc feel bad about killing the animal it's eating? Not a bit. So when someone is said to be crying crocodile tears, it means they are not really sorry or feeling sad about something, but only pretending to be.

Gobbledygook!

Why is a turkey called a turkey? It all dates back to when Christopher Columbus (1451–1506) first set foot on American soil, accompanied by his Hebrew interpreter. In Hebrew, the word for peacock is *tuki*—which is what the interpreter called the fan-tailed wild bird that has been known as a turkey ever since.

The last word in some editions of the Merriam-Webster Dictionary is *zyzzva*, meaning "the last word"!

Comma Knowledge

Punctuation can mean the difference between life and death! Maria Fyodorovna (1848–1928), wife of Russia's Emperor Alexander III (1845–1894), transposed a comma and saved a life. She was handed paperwork that said, "Pardon impossible, send to Siberia." She read, instead, "Pardon, impossible send to Siberia." The convict, who was released immediately, walked out of prison a free man.

RIPLEY FILE: 7.7.91

Believe It or Not! In some early Aztec wall paintings, people are pictured with speech balloons—just like the cartoons of today!

Different Strokes

The *Chung-wen ta-t'zu-tien*, an encyclopedic dictionary of the Chinese language, is 40 volumes long and contains 50,000 characters, including one character that requires 64 different brushstrokes. To read a Chinese newspaper, readers have to know at least 7,000 characters!

EXTRA! EXTRA!

Tunnel Vision

Just about everyone has heard of the exploits of Robin Hood, that legendary British outlaw who stole from the rich to give to the poor. In one tale, he gets trapped inside a church with the Sheriff of Nottingham in hot pursuit. Legend has it that the hero escaped through a secret passageway that led to tunnels under the prison. A recently discovered tunnel under the Nottingham streets is just one more bit of evidence that Robin Hood was an actual person and not just a legend.

Making a Stink

In August 2003, residents of Lichtenwoerth, Austria, petitioned the local government to rename their town Stinkendorf—or roughly in English, Stinksville. It seems the pig population there outnumbers human citizens five to one. So if you're planning to visit anytime soon, you'd better take a clothespin for your nose!

Odd Lots

Jean François Vernetti of Switzerland has an unusual claim to fame. He has amassed the world's largest collection of hotel "Do Not Disturb" signs. Stranger still is the collection of Niek Vermeulen of Holland who has accumulated 3,240 airplane barf bags.

Mad Scramble

At the annual Marshmallow Drop held the Saturday before Easter in Miami Shores, Florida, 30,000 marshmallows are dropped from a helicopter for children to collect.

Windshield Viper

In September 2003, Marko Obradovic, of Berane, Montenegro, was driving to work with three passengers when a snake poked its head out of a dashboard vent. Obradovic slammed on the brakes, and the businessmen abandoned the car. Since neither the police nor the towing company would go near the car, it stayed where it was for more than two hours, bringing rush hour traffic to a standstill. Desperate to clear the traffic, a clever commuter set fire to an old piece of carpet and shoved it beneath the car. It worked. The snake was smoked out, and, finally, everyone could get to work.

Hammerheads

In Portugal, there is an all-night celebration in which participants feast on sardines and strike each other on the head with plastic hammers.

Signs of Aging

The Keita tribe of Africa has ten different symbols for "woman." Determining which one is used depends on the woman's age.

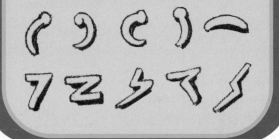

Chinese Know-how

In America, *ch'uan fa*, a Chinese form of fighting, was mistakenly called kung fu, which simply means to have a skill in or to be skillful at anything.

No Baby on Board

Instead of landing instructions, pilots approaching England's Luton Airport in the spring of 2003 heard a baby's cries coming loud and clear over their radios. After 12 hours of detective work, airline officials discovered that a baby monitor in a home nearby was broadcasting the cries of little Freya Spratley to the cockpits of approaching aircraft.

2

DOLLARS AND SENSE

MAD MARKETING

A Swell Idea

Expectant British moms now have a new way to earn some extra cash. In England, Tomy, the Japanese toy company, is renting space on their swollen tummies to advertise MicroBabies, the company's latest product.

Making Headway

Cunning Stunts, an extremely imaginative marketing agency in Great Britain, has come up with a new way to advertise their clients' products—using students' foreheads as billboards! They are offering students the equivalent of about $155 per week to wear a transfer made of nontoxic vegetable dye that displays a corporate logo on their forehead for a minimum of three hours a day.

MOO-VABLE SIGNS

In 1989, Charles Wilkinson, a real estate developer and dairy farmer, used the sides of his cows to advertise a housing development because road signs were illegal in Kemblesville, Pennsylvania.

Square Deal!

In 1955, the Quaker Oats company came up with a unique advertising scheme to capitalize on a popular TV show it sponsored called *Sergeant Preston of the Yukon*. The company bought 19.11 acres in the Yukon territory from the Canadian government for $10,000, then placed legal deeds to one square inch of the land inside 21 million boxes of Puffed Rice and Puffed Wheat.

A Real Shoe-in!

A French shoe company advertised their product by using a car shaped like a lace-up boot.

Making a Stink

A rose by any other name might smell as sweet, but it just might not sell the product. An Estée Lauder perfume called Country Mist had disappointing sales in Germany because the German word *mist* is slang for manure!

MONEY MADNESS

Made of Money

In 1930, a 10-foot-long, 8-foot-high shoe made with six million shredded one-dollar bills that had been taken out of circulation was used as a float in an American Legion parade in Boston, Massachusetts.

Beetlemania

How much money is a beetle worth? A beetle bug, that is. Would you believe that the president of a company in Tokyo, Japan, paid $90,000 for one? No, the man is not going buggy. He is simply a bug collector who thought that the rare 3-inch stag beetle, also known as a "black diamond," would be an invaluable addition to his collection. He prefers to remain anonymous to prevent thieves from stealing his prized beetle. Believe It!

ANT-I HERO

For 58 years, at a cost of $2,813,000, Rani Bhawani (1748–1806) of Nator, India, had honey poured into every ant hole in the country so that no ant would ever go hungry.

Child's Play

Don't throw away your old toys. You never know what that favorite doll or action figure might be worth in years to come. When they first came out in 1963, G. I. Joe figures were sold for $4.00. In 1999, Matt Babek paid $14,000 for one. Instead of playing with it, however, he keeps it in a bank vault.

Made a Killing

In 1861, George Grant, a Scottish cloth merchant who was living in London, England, at the time, read in *The London Times* newspaper that Prince Albert, husband of Queen Victoria, was ill. Knowing that if the prince should die, every building in England would be draped in black fabric as a sign of mourning, Grant promptly bought up every yard of black crepe he could find. When the prince died, Grant sold the crepe and made a profit of $250,000.

RIPLEY FILE: 9.29.65

Dirty pool! After Maximilian II Emanuel (1662–1726), ruler of Bavaria, lost the battle of Blenheim in 1704, he was in trouble. When it was discovered that he'd also lost $3,600,000 of the Bavarian treasury's money playing billiards, he was promptly forced out and banished from the country for ten years.

CASH AND CARRY

Them's the Breaks!

In the 1700s, many European banks gave out small porcelain "borrower's tiles" to their customers. Like credit cards, these tiles were imprinted with the owner's name, credit limit, and the name of the bank. Each time the customer wanted to borrow money, the tile was presented to the bank teller, who would compare the imprinted credit limit on the tile with how much the customer had already borrowed. If the borrower was over the limit, the teller broke the tile on the spot. That's why people say they're broke when they're out of money!

No Bones to Pick

In 1968, Ella Wendell of New York left a will bequeathing her $30,000,000 fortune to Toby, her pet poodle!

Buggin'

The Roman poet Virgil once paid the equivalent of $100,000 to provide a lavish funeral for a housefly and buried it in a special mausoleum on his estate.

Penny-pincher

Sylvester Neal of Auburn, Washington, had been socking away pennies for more than 40 years. When he moved from Alaska in July 2001, he decided it would be easier to cash them in than transport them to his new home—a wise move, considering he had 792,141 pennies, which weighed 5 tons, stashed away in his basement!

The Cat That Got the Cream

When Margaret Layne of London, England, died in 2002, she left her entire estate, valued at the equivalent of $937,000, to her cat. Tinker is now living the good life in his own house, dining on fish, bowls of cream, and all the delicacies money can buy. Not bad for a cat who was once a stray!

GOLDEN RETRIEVER

In 1997, a Doberman pinscher in El Paso, Texas, dug up a bag of money that had been buried in the ground and forgotten. Inside the bag was $13,500!

RIPLEY FILE: 1.24.65

Strong backing! In the 11th century, Masud I, ruler of the Ghazna region of what is now Afghanistan, always carried the entire state treasury—as much as $150,000,000—on the backs of 3,000 personally trained camels. Each camel obeyed a different password known only to Masud, who would give a creditor the correct password for a camel carrying exactly the sum he was to collect. Only when the right password was uttered would a camel permit itself to be led away and unloaded of its precious cargo.

THE SKY'S THE LIMIT

A Real Gem

In 1997, Diamond Cutters International created a model car for Chrysler Plymouth to launch their new Prowler roadster. Called the Gem Prowler, the 12-inch-long replica was cut from the world's largest amethyst, weighing 15,000 carats. With a windshield carved out of crystal and studded with diamonds, the Gem Prowler is a steal at $200,000.

On the Fly

How much would you pay for a pigeon? Would a couple of thousand dollars seem like too much? The average racing pigeon flies at speeds of 45 to 50 miles per hour. It is not uncommon for one released 500 miles from its home at dawn to arrive back by nightfall. These pedigreed birds are bred especially for racing and can cost thousands of dollars. Invincible Spirit, who beat 27,157 other pigeons to win the 1992 Barcelona International Race, was purchased for more than $160,000, the most money ever paid for a bird.

DIAMOND GIRL

In 1999, to celebrate the 40th anniversary of the introduction of the Barbie doll, the Mattel toy company created a diamond-studded Barbie valued at more than $82,000!

All You Need Is ...

In November 2003, the handwritten lyrics penned by the late John Lennon for the song "Nowhere Man" sold for $455,000. On another occasion, Beatles fan Brian Faylor of Washington, D.C., paid $18,000 for Paul McCartney's birth certificate.

A Big Bill!

A handwritten copy of the first ten Constitutional amendments, also known as the Bill of Rights, was recovered by the FBI in March 2003 when an antiques dealer in Connecticut tried to sell it to an undercover agent. This precious document was stolen from North Carolina's capitol building 138 years ago, and officials have been on the lookout for it ever since. One of 14 copies commissioned in 1789 by George Washington, it's currently valued at about $30,000,000!

RIPLEY FILE:
5.5.54

Lovebirds! To appease the gods, Khanderao, maharaja of Baroda, India, from 1856 to 1870, invited all the notables in his kingdom to 42 marriage ceremonies—each for a pair of pigeons! The cost of the festivities? $2,000,000!

EXTRA! EXTRA!

Shipshape

Stephen Girard (1750–1831) of Philadelphia, Pennsylvania, started his career as a cabin boy on a ship. By 1814, he had become successful enough as a banker to offer a $5,000,000 loan to the hard-pressed United States government.

A Lot of Lettuce!

Raymond Blanc, chef of Le Manoir aux Quat' Saisons restaurant in Oxford, England, created the Florette Sea and Earth Salad to launch Florette's National Salad Week. The salad starts with a bed of greens and includes a round "basket" woven of zucchini, red peppers, and potato, which is surrounded by tidbits of Almas caviar (once reserved for Russian tsars), Beluga caviar, crab, lobster, and truffles, all dusted with grated truffles and gold leaf. The price of this delicacy? The equivalent of just over $1,000.

Heads I Win— Tails You Lose

An American penny issued in 1784 had a portrait of George Washington—on both sides.

Cash Tip

In 2002, the hottest nail fashion in Toronto, Canada, involved cutting up money, applying the pieces to the fingernails, and adding a coat of acrylic.

Money Laundering

At the Sanwa Bank in Tokyo, Japan, banknotes are sanitized before being dispensed by automated teller machines that are made out of plastic that's been treated to resist bacteria.

Spooky!

Tourists come from far and wide to meet the dozen or so witches of Deda, Romania, who cast spells for people hoping to get revenge, achieve success, or gain some other favor—as long as they pay! Now that the mayor has begun to tax magic spells, they'll have to give a portion of the money to the town. The taxes go to people in the village who are handicapped or underprivileged.

Plastic Cash

In April 2000, the government of Brazil issued banknotes made of plastic.

The Money Ran Out

A bronze coin circulated 1,900 years ago in ancient Gaul was shaped like the hindquarters of a pig—including the legs—and was worth exactly the price of a ham.

Go Fish!

In 1992, a 352-pound tuna sold at an auction in Japan for $69,273.30.

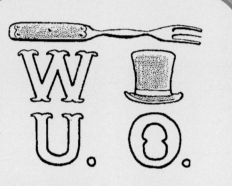

Pay Up!

A rebus is a riddle that is made up of pictures. One rebus popular in the United States 100 years ago reads: Fork over what you owe.

For Pet-icular Pets

Animal Manors, a company in New York, builds custom-made pet houses, including a French chateau that sells for $8,047—a bargain when you compare it to a bejeweled Egyptian temple priced at $124,000.

3

BEASTIES

Dog-gone Amazing!

Skidboot liked to chase the neighbors' chickens and chew up everything in sight. One day his owner, David Hartwig of Quinlan, Texas, decided to teach his dog some manners. Skidboot learned new behaviors so fast, Hartwig thought he was a genius. Hartwig wasn't alone. Now Skidboot wows rodeo and TV audiences all over the country. He even has his own book and video. In one trick, Skidboot holds a biscuit between his teeth while Hartwig reads the ingredients listed on the package—and Skidboot doesn't chomp down on the biscuit until he hears the word *beef*!

Mental Floss

A cockatoo named Rikki doesn't have any teeth, but she seems to think she does. After watching her owner, Donna Felsing, floss each morning, Rikki decided it looked like fun. So she picked up a box of dental floss, broke off a piece, and pulled it through her beak with her claws. Felsing says Rikki will do anything for attention, and now will floss her beak on command.

ON A ROLL

Betty Ottaviano thought her house was haunted when she saw a stroller crossing the floor by itself. When she realized her pet turtle was pushing it, she gave him a treat. Now he pushes the stroller whenever he wants a snack!

Pig-casso

Since he first picked up a brush in 1998, Smithfield, a Vietnamese potbelly pig, has produced paintings so lovely that they've fetched hundreds of dollars each on eBay. To date, the productive pig has earned $20,000 through the sale of his art, all of which has been donated to charities.

RIPLEY FILE: 11.25.66

Trunk show! In 1854, a British animal trainer named Cooke taught two circus elephants to sit at a table, eat dinner using forks, and sip wine from goblets.

Purr-fect Eti-cat

When Tessa the cat eats, she sits at the table. It all started in the mid-1990s, when Faye Murrell's grown children left home. The dinner table seemed empty without them, so Murrell taught Tessa some table manners. The clever cat learned how to use a fork in no time. When noodles are served, Tessa chows down with chopsticks, and on special occasions, she eats ice cream with a spoon.

MIXED COMPANY

Watertight

In 1998, Dan Heath of Medford, Oregon, could barely believe his eyes when he saw Chino, his golden retriever, standing over a fishpond nose to nose with Falstaff, an orange-and-black carp. Each day, Chino sprints out to the backyard, peers into the water, and waits. Within seconds, Falstaff pops up and the two gently touch noses. Heath doesn't know how or why they became friends, but it's obvious to anyone who sees them that their friendship is watertight!

Lionhearted

An oryx is an African antelope with horns up to 48 inches long. Lions love them—at mealtime, that is! That's why scientists are finding the behavior of a lioness named Kamuniak puzzling, to say the least. Kamuniak lives on the Samburu National Reserve in Kenya, where, since January 1992, she has taken to scaring off mother oryx and adopting their babies. She hunts food for them and protects them from other lions, cheetahs, and leopards. No lyin'!

HAREBRAINED!

Lucky, a cat owned by Jennifer Anderson of London, Ohio, adopted and nursed a baby rabbit.

RIPLEY FILE: 11.14.64

Hot dog! In 1936, a firehouse dog named Blackie saved a cat from a burning building by carrying it down a ladder.

Udder-ly Amazing!

Cattle and sheep usually don't mix, but when a group of lambs was penned in the same pasture with cattle, the two species bonded so much that the cattle actually protected the sheep from predators.

Milkmaid

Sometimes animals raised in captivity lose their natural instincts. That happened in 2001 at a zoo in Uzbekistan when a Siberian tiger rejected her own cub. Luckily, a stray dog named Klava had more than her share of motherly love to go around. Klava nursed the tiger cub for 30 days, until it was strong enough to start eating meat. Without Klava's care, the cub, a member of an endangered species, most certainly would have died.

TO THE RESCUE

Horse Sense

Rosie the sheepdog had been missing for days. It turned out she'd slipped through an open gate into a neighbor's pasture and later couldn't get past the electrified fence to get out. Luckily, a miniature horse named Goodbar was there. Sensing that Rosie was scared, Goodbar trotted over and began to lick her fur. Then he stood over her to keep her away from the electric fence. Goodbar's owner, Jennifer Groters, couldn't coax the dog from Goodbar's side, so the horse took over. For a full 45 minutes, he patiently nudged the frightened dog toward Groters—so that she could scoop her up and take her home.

Out of the Woods

One cold winter day in 1999, 36-year-old Michael Miller took Sadie, his English setter, out hunting. Suddenly, a third of a mile into the woods, Miller had a heart attack. He called Sadie with a whistle, then fell to the ground. Unable to walk, Miller held on to Sadie's collar—and the 45-pound dog dragged her 180-pound owner, now semiconscious, all the way home. Miller's wife called for an ambulance, and he was rushed to the hospital for emergency surgery. Without Sadie's help, Miller might never have made it out of the woods.

Mighty Rat

Fido the rat was sleeping peacefully when he was awakened by the smell of smoke. He broke out of his cage, and instead of running out of the house to safety, he scampered through flames and up the stairs to the second floor where Lisa Gumbley and her daughters, nine-year-old Megan and three-year-old Shannon, were sleeping. He scratched and scratched at their door, refusing to leave until they awoke. Happily, the family escaped without injury, but if it hadn't been for their brave little pet, mother and daughters surely would have perished in the fire.

BRAVE HEART

In 1996, Fizo, a dog in Sydney, Australia, was awarded the RSPCA Purple Cross for bravery after saving three children from a deadly snake.

Bull Session

Donald Mottram of Carmarthen, West Wales, owes his life to his favorite cow, Daisy. In 1966, Mottram was in his pasture when he was attacked by a 3,000-pound bull. The snorting beast charged, knocked Mottram to the ground, and stomped on him. The farmer lost consciousness. An hour and half later, a dazed Mottram awoke to find that his herd of cows had formed a protective ring around him. Led by Daisy, they continued to shield him from the bull as he crawled away to safety.

RIPLEY FILE: 8.8.71

Porpoise with a purpose! For a period of 20 years, from 1790 to 1810, a snow-white albino dolphin named Hatteras Jack guided every ship in and out of Hatteras Inlet, off the coast of North Carolina, and never lost a single vessel.

PAMPERED PETS

Up a Tree

Charles McClain is the proud owner of Tree Cat, a real-life scaredy-cat. He found the cat three years ago, crying from his perch at the top of a 60-foot-high oak tree. McClain tried everything to coax him down, but Tree Cat wouldn't budge. Now, McClain gets up at six o'clock every morning and climbs a ladder to give the cat his breakfast. This routine suits Tree Cat just fine, because he still hasn't left the tree! But why should he? Tree Cat has it made in the shade with his own custom-made home, complete with a soft bed, a front porch, and a deck where he eats his meals.

CREATURE COMFORTS

At Miami's Mayfair House Hotel, dogs get their own bed and "amenity package," including gourmet dog biscuits. If that's not enough, their owners can order up a four-course meal from doggie room service!

Shady Characters

A German company called Dog Goes is having a hard time keeping up with the demand for their product. What do they make? Sunglasses for dogs.

Mutant Menagerie

Take a good look at the animals in Paul Springer's pasture and you're bound to notice something odd. Here and there you'll find a pig with an extra snout, a pair of donkeys joined at the head, a cow with some extra legs, and maybe even a two-headed calf. Springer's Wisconsin farm is home to some of the most astonishing livestock you'll ever lay eyes on.

Springer developed a soft spot for mutant animals when a steer named Beauregard was born on his farm. Most farmers would have destroyed a steer with two extra legs sprouting from its shoulders, but not Springer. He developed a warm relationship with the steer, whose affectionate nature soon established him as a beloved family pet.

Since then, Springer has actively sought out animals that would otherwise be destroyed because of high upkeep costs. Springer keeps his mutant menagerie in a special paddock free of wires and branches that might snag delicate extra limbs. They require little special care, except during the first shaky months of their lives when survival is doubtful. Corrective surgery is usually too risky because the extra parts are often fused directly to the animal's spinal cord.

Besides his odd-inary herd, Springer keeps 150 normal head of cattle as well as miniature burros. He feeds the animals candy in addition to hay and lavishes them all with great care—whether they have spare parts or not.

EARNING THEIR KEEP

Monkey Business

An ancient Egyptian painting indicates that 4,000 years ago, baboons were taught to harvest figs. Today, in Thailand, pigtailed macaque monkeys are trained to scurry up trees to harvest coconuts.

Bearing Up

Each year, a great number of bears are destroyed for coming too close to "people" areas. Now, thanks to the Wind River Bear Institute's "Partners-In-Life" program and their Karelian Bear Dogs, fewer bears all around the world will be killed. Wildlife biologist and program founder Carrie Hunt (left) has trained the dogs to help her teach bears to stay away from places where they aren't welcome. Bears crossing into human-inhabited areas are surprised with firecrackers, rubber bullets, and fierce barking. Hunt's crew and the dogs chase the bears to a pre-set boundary. As soon as the bears are out of the "people" area, the chase ends and the barking stops. It doesn't take long for most bears to get the picture. Hunt and her crew also teach people how to avoid attracting bears—so everybody wins!

FLEECE POLICE

In 1996, the town of Culembourg, Netherlands, let six sheep loose in the streets to slow commuter traffic during the morning and evening rush hours.

RIPLEY FILE: 3.12.94

Paw power! **In England during the 1400s, terriers were trained to run inside revolving cages to turn a crank that fired a spit.**

Scratch and Sniff

In 2002, Russian officials, who were having quite a problem sniffing out caviar smugglers, got just the help they needed from a secret agent named Rusik. What made this agent so good at his job? Rusik was a cat with a nose for fish!

Bee-ware!

A honeybee weighs an ounce or less, while an elephant weighs several tons. Yet, bees have been known to send a whole herd of elephants stampeding off in fright. Why? Because the inside of an elephant's trunk and its soft underbelly are extremely vulnerable to stings. Now, scientists in Kenya are putting beehives in trees to keep them from being trampled on by the elephants. This would also protect elephants, which have been shot by angry farmers, eager to keep them from destroying their property. Most everyone agrees that controlling elephants with bees is better than shooting them.

EXTRA! EXTRA!

Groupies

A herd of elk is called a *gang*. A group of jellyfish is called a *smuck*. A group of ferrets is called a *business*. A group of kangaroos is called a *mob*, a group of apes is called a *shrewdness*, and a group of a rhinoceroses is called a *crash*.

How Sweet It Is!

For those who like to get up close and personal with their pets, a new product is about to sweeten the experience. With odor-fighting ingredients such as parsley, rosemary, and green-tea extract, Yip Yap Mints promise to banish doggie breath—at least for a little while. Soon to be widely available, Pit'r Pat breath fresheners will do the same thing for cats.

Yum!

Stephen Hoy of the United States has invented edible greeting cards for animals.

Brain Power

In 1938, a popular attraction at the State Fair of Texas was Captain E. C. Lower's Bozo, the Mind-Reading Dog. Bozo could accurately bark out the number, dates, and denominations of coins held in audience members' hands, the number of rings on their fingers, and any number his master was thinking.

Eeeeek!

Every year, Nebraska Wesleyan University hosts The Event Formerly Known as the Rat Olympics. Rats compete in such events as the long jump, weight lifting, and the 5-foot rope climb.

I'm Home!

The problem with the average pet door is that, instead of your pet, the occasional chipmunk or squirrel just might come waltzing in. Now, instead of a pet door, you can try a new product called the Pet-2-Ring Doorbell. The device comes with a video showing owners how to use food rewards to train their pets to push a lever—which rings chimes inside the house! Then owners know that their pet is waiting by the door, ready to come inside.

Lousy Job

The marmoset, a tiny primate found in South and Central America, is worn in the hair of the Saterei people to pick out head lice.

Knight in Shining Dog Fur

Bernard, a Saint Bernard dog from Eagle, Canada, rescued Jack Grover from a car wreck by pulling him through the windshield and licking his face until help arrived.

Deer-ly Beloved

Reindeer are so vital to the lives of the Chukchi people of Siberia that their language has 26 different words for reindeer.

Cat-Bird

A cat owned by the Gagen family of Schenectady, New York, adopted and raised two baby chicks.

Having a Ball

Moja, an African elephant at the Miami Metro Zoo in Florida, loves sports. Among his favorites are bowling, football, and softball.

4

NICE GOING!

RADICAL ROADSTERS

Batteries Included

The 25-foot-long White Lightning electric streamliner (below) was designed by Dempsey World Record Associates (DWRA), a group that really knows how to think outside the box. Knowing that conventional car batteries would be too heavy for the race car, DWRA decided to try ordinary flashlight batteries—6,040 of them to be exact! Did they work? You bet! On October 22, 1999, White Lightning set a world land speed record for electric cars of just over 245 miles per hour.

By Land or by Sea

On land, the convertible Aquada Sports Amphibian (above) can be driven at up to 100 miles per hour. Drive it into a river, flick a switch to retract the wheels, and in a mere ten seconds, the car becomes a jet-powered boat that can skim across the water at more than 30 miles per hour!

UPSTART

In 1992, the Delta Beetle, a car with triangular wheels that could climb stairs, won the gold medal at the 16th annual Idea Olympics in Toyota, Japan.

RIPLEY FILE: 10.27.63

Scent-sational! **A carriage built in 1649 by Hans Hautsch of Nürnberg, Germany, could be pedaled at a speed of one mile per hour—and at the same time, spray perfume on passersby through an atomizer in the dragon's head mounted on the front.**

McFuel

When Abraham Noe-Hays wants to fuel up his car, he pulls up to a fast-food restaurant, sticks a hose into the fryer-fat dumpster, and siphons free used vegetable oil through a filter into his fuel tank. Noe-Hays cares about the environment, so he was really excited to find out about this fragrant alternative to fossil fuels. He bought a fuel converter kit, spent a weekend turning his 1989 Volkswagen Jetta from a car that runs on diesel fuel to one that runs on vegetable oil, and was ready to roll.

It's in the Bag

When Mazda held a design contest in 1991, one of the company's engineers had a brainstorm. Instead of having to wait in line at an airport to get a bus or a taxi, wouldn't it be great to just collect your suitcase, pop it open, and drive away in it? The result was the Mazda Suitcase car—a car that's so small it fits inside a suitcase. It can be assembled in about 20 seconds, and goes up to 27 miles per hour.

1
2
3

Go!

MAD MAKEOVERS

Finmobile

Looking at Tom Kennedy's "Ripper the Friendly Shark," it's hard to tell that it's actually a 1982 Nissan Sentra. The car has been transformed into a replica of a shark on wheels. Inside, rubber fish hanging from the ceiling give off an eerie glow in the fluorescent light, creating the impression that the passengers have been swallowed by a real shark!

Psychedelic Relic

What better way to go for a magical mystery tour than in this 1965 Phantom V Rolls-Royce that once belonged to John Lennon? Not everyone liked it. In London, a woman once whacked the car with her umbrella while shouting, "You swine! You swine! How dare you do this to a Rolls-Royce?" In 1985, the car was purchased for $2,299,000 by Canadian entrepreneur Jim Pattison, the owner of Ripley's International, who later donated it to the Royal British Columbia Museum.

COMMON CENTS!

In 1978, George D. King of Pompano Beach, Florida, finished decorating his van with 48,773 pennies.

Turns on a Dime

Covering a car with 25,172 dimes is not everyone's idea of fun, but the former owner of one 1973 Honda did it anyway—and he certainly got his money's worth as far as attention! Better yet, the car, which bears the Arizona license plate "Hondime," is guaranteed to hold its value. All those dimes add up to a total of $2,517.20.

RIPLEY FILE:
8.19.2000

All dolled up! Arlene Lambert of Toronto, Canada, drives a car that is covered with hundreds of plastic baby dolls.

Real Corker

Jan Elftman collected thousands of corks during the 13 years that she worked as a member of the waitstaff in an Italian restaurant. What did she do with them all? She decorated her pickup truck, of course!

491·KHJ

PEDAL POWER

Family Cycle

Roger Dumas labored for more than 20 years to build a bicycle that would transport his entire extended family. The result, a two-tiered, 140-foot-long bicycle, incorporates parts from 150 other bicycles. At a family reunion in 2000, all 55 members of the Dumas family, aged 3 to 76, climbed onto the bicycle and rode it a total of 3,236 feet 6 inches—over half a mile!

Training Bike

In 1999, the National Bicycle Industrial Company and the East Japan Railway Company got together to make the Traincle 6500 folding bicycle. The Traincle (from *train* plus *bicycle*) takes up very little space when folded up—it will even fit inside a suitcase—and weighs just over 14 pounds, making it a breeze for commuters to carry onto the train.

No Leg Work

Bicycle riders traveling between Helmond and Eindhoven in the Netherlands may one day get to ride in a special 8-mile-long tunnel that contains huge electric fans that will push them along at 30 miles per hour.

RIPLEY FILE: 8.10.41

Wheely fast dogs! **In 1875, a Frenchman named Guitu invented the *cynosphere*, a tricycle that could go up to six miles per hour—powered by two dogs running inside the back wheels.**

WHEEL-Y LITTLE

For a very short trip, you might consider trying an 8-inch-high unicycle created by Signar Berglund of Sweden. Trick rider Peter Rosendahl has ridden it a grand total of 38 feet 1.1 inches.

Sew Clever

In the 1930s and 1940s, Joe Steinlauf created whimsical bicycles made out of unusual materials, such as a brass bed (above) and a sewing machine.

Pedal Picker

In 1981, Ray Nelson of San Jose, California, built a fully functional motorcycle in the shape of an electric guitar, which he's ridden from California to New York City.

ZANY ZONE

Desk Jockey

Edd China of London, England, will always go the distance to raise money for Comic Relief, his favorite charity. His Casual Lofa, a motorized sofa with a pizza pan for a steering wheel has already covered 6,219 miles. Now China has designed and built another one-of-a-kind vehicle called the Hot Desk (above), which he drove 900 miles in March 2003 to raise money for the charity.

Just Humming Along

The first High Mobility Multipurpose Wheeled Vehicles—Humvees for short—were developed for the United States Army. When tested over 600,000 miles of rough terrain in extreme temperatures, they passed with flying colors. Now you can experience the thrill of riding in a combat vehicle without the combat. Comfortably seating 16 adults, the Humvee H2 Limo sports six flat screen TVs, a CD stereo, strobes, neon and laser mood lighting, two fish tanks, and a fireplace. Rent one and you can ride to your destination in style over rough terrain or not.

SPACEY!

Paul Moller, an engineer in Davis, California, designs and builds full-sized flying saucers that can hover 40 feet above the ground.

Flights of Fancy

The first Flügtag—which means "flying day"—took place in Austria in 1991. Since then, Flügtags have been springing up all over the place. These flaky festivals are giving creative folk who dream of flying a chance to really take off. Contestants, who build their own outrageous aircraft, launch themselves from a flat runway that ends in a 20-foot drop over water. Whoever travels the farthest wins. While they rarely set records for distance, handmade flying machines sporting names such as *Murphy's Law* and *Kid Icarus* are delightful, ingenious monuments to the bizarre.

RIPLEY FILE: 10.25.90

Venetian vehicle! Livio de Marchi of Venice, Italy, built a 3,300-pound wooden scale model of a 1937 Jaguar powered by a 20-horsepower engine. Because it's made of wood, the vehicle floats like a boat and can cruise the city's canals.

Spooky Sports Car

Retired deputy sheriff Roger Fox of Fairborn, Ohio, took four years to assemble his one-of-a-kind coffin-car from two caskets and parts from various 1960s "muscle" cars. Fox loves it so much that he plans to be buried in it!

EXTRA! EXTRA!

It's About Time!

Dave Moore of Rosemead, California, built an 8-foot-high metal unicycle in 1989 that was based on designs drawn 500 years ago by Leonardo da Vinci.

Double Take

In 1986, Craig Hosking of Bountiful, Utah, added an extra set of wheels on top of his airplane so he could take off and land upside down as well as right side up!

Flying Solo

A company in Japan has developed a personal helicopter that holds one rider. It can fly for up to 60 minutes at a speed of 62 miles per hour! If you're interested, it's currently on the market with a full assembly kit, and sells for $30,000.

Red Alert

Until 1896, mechanical vehicles in England could not be driven faster than four miles per hour, and they had to be preceded by a man carrying a red flag. The reason? To warn others in the street to exercise caution. Today, the phrase "to put up a red flag" is a warning to proceed with caution.

MAKE WAY! MAKE WAY!

Steal This!

Invented by a British company, the AutoPod can be hidden under the driveway, a patch of grass, or even the garden. Once installed, just park the car in the pod, push a button, and your car is lowered into the ground where it remains safe and sound till you're ready to go again.

Big Wheels

An eight-man tricycle built in New England in 1896 weighed 2,500 pounds, was 17 feet long, and had wheels that were 11 feet in diameter.

Let's Roll!

Motor-driven roller skates, invented by Alphonse Constantini in 1906, could travel at 40 miles per hour. Today, consumers who are looking for a convenient high-speed thrill can purchase Roller Sneakers—sneakers and skates all rolled into one!

Bus-zarre!

A group of people in Sao Paolo, Brazil, have an unusual obsession: They love buses. Members of the Bus Worshippers Club spend whole days at bus stations watching buses, discussing buses, and photographing the people who ride them! Now the group is planning a journey from Chile to Alaska. How are they traveling? By bus, of course!

Heads Up

In 1900, a horseless carriage designed by Uriah Smith of Battle Creek, Michigan, had a model of a horse's head mounted at the front so that it would not scare real horses.

5

OVER THE TOP

QUIRKY WORK

The Dark Side

Louise Hose (below) loves to explore places where no one has ever been before. That's why her job—exploring and mapping caves—is the perfect work for her. Hose and her colleagues have to wear respirators when they explore a cavern named La Cueva de Villa Luz in Tabasco, Mexico, because poisonous gas fills the air! There, they study bacteria that live in slimy colonies, dubbed "snottites," that drip sulfuric acid.

Spider Men

Australian Stuart Douglas (above) "milks" tarantulas for their venom, which he sells to scientists who are researching the use of spider venom in fighting various illnesses. Douglas only has about 300 tarantulas, but Chuck Kristensen of Arizona shares his home with about 50,000 spiders and milks them every week. Since spider venom is already being used in medicines that combat heart disease, a thimbleful from some species can fetch hundreds of dollars. The catch is that it can take months to produce a single thimbleful.

BLOOD TEST

Several companies in China require applicants for sales positions to have type O or type B blood because it is believed these blood types indicate stable and pleasant personalities.

Runway Rescue

Each year, from May to October, retired Earth science teacher Bob Leporati drives to New York's JFK airport five days a week. No, he's not a pilot and he's not a jet-setter either. He goes to the airport to work with his pet falcon, Konner. Together, they perform a very important job—helping to keep the runways safe for takeoff.

Bird-related airplane crashes are more common than most people think—and it just so happens that the largest colony of laughing gulls on the East Coast nests on the marsh right next to JFK. In 1975, a jumbo jet crashed while trying to take off when several seagulls were sucked into its engine. Since then, workers at the airport have tried a variety of high-tech methods to scare birds away from the runways. To date, no method has worked as well as using falcons.

Falcons are extremely intelligent birds of prey, and many birds, including seagulls, are instinctively afraid of them. For six months of the year, Konner lives in a special section of the airport called the mews, along with 16 other working birds. His trainer, Leporati, is an expert in the ancient sport of falconry and has trained Konner to respond to a lure by going into attack mode. The gulls can't get away fast enough! Since people like Leporati and birds like Konner have been on the job, JFK has not had a single bird-related accident.

FUNNY BUSINESS

Tops in His Field

Every six months, Tom Silliman, secured with nothing more than a harness attached to a safety line, climbs to the very top of the antenna on New York's Empire State Building. Why? To change the lightbulb in the skyscraper's aviation beacon, which warns low-flying aircraft to steer clear. An electrical engineer whose company builds antenna towers at the tops of skyscrapers, Silliman is very comfortable with heights. Good thing! The Empire State Building's beacon is more than 1,454 feet above the streets!

Class Act

Dr. George Plitnick, a physics professor at Frostburg State University in Maryland, has found a way to get and keep his students' attention—by dressing up like a wizard and teaching a class called "The Science of Harry Potter." With nothing more than a few props, such as a petri dish and a bit of liquid nitrogen, Plitnick attempts to answer such questions as "Can objects really be levitated?" No wonder there's a waiting list to get into this wizard's class!

HUMAN ALARM CLOCK

Mary Smith of London, England, earned money by shooting peas at the bedroom windows of people who hired her to wake them up.

RIPLEY FILE: 12.27.60

Switch doctor!
According to cultural tradition in Angola, Africa, a witch doctor who wishes to quit his profession must wear a mask day and night for a whole year before he can resign. Afterward, he will take on a new identity and be known by a new name.

Quackery

In January 2003, the Peabody Hotel had a job opening. The requirements? Someone who has a way with people—and ducks! Daniel Fox fit the bill. As the new duck handler at the Peabody, an elegant landmark located in Memphis, Tennessee, Fox gets to lead the resident ducks twice a day on their world-famous march from their rooftop home to the hotel's fountain in the lobby.

REALLY OUT THERE!

Feline Envy

Actress Sarah Bernhardt once consulted a doctor about having the tail of a tiger grafted to the base of her spine—though she did not actually go through with it.

What a Gas!

When Joseph Pujol, a French entertainer in the late 1800s, did his act, theater owners made sure there was a doctor on hand to revive all the people who fainted from laughing so hard. Known as Le Pétomane (roughly translated as "fartiste"), Pujol did imitations of cannon fire, machine guns, musical scores, and thunder—all by passing gas!

Hangin' Out

There's standing room only at a popular hangout in Tokyo, Japan. Why? The band there plays their instruments while hanging upside down! Each member of Johnny Against Gravity, a five-piece rockabilly band, hangs from steel girders by his ankles. It's a good idea to get there on time, however, because the band can only play that way for 30 to 40 minutes before passing out!

Cowboy Underpants

In New York City, it is not unusual to see people who are a little offbeat. What is unusual is for passersby to notice them—but when Robert John Burck takes to the streets, people actually stop and stare. That's because this street performer, who calls himself The Naked Cowboy, plays his guitar and sings, wearing nothing but a cowboy hat, cowboy boots, and his tighty-whities!

DOUBLE VISION

Comedian Charlie Chaplin (1889–1977) once entered a Charlie Chaplin lookalike contest—and lost!

RIPLEY FILE: 8.24.69

Cage fright! The brilliant French actor Charles Dullin (1885–1949) received his dramatic training by reciting poetry daily for seven years—while inside a cage filled with lions!

EXTREME MAKEOVERS

Hold That Tiger!

Dennis Avner, who calls himself Catman, has always thought of himself as a tiger in a man's body. After more than $100,000 dollars worth of plastic surgery and tattoos to make himself look like a tiger, the San Diego computer programmer was still not satisfied. So he had his teeth filed into sharp points, dyed his hair orange, had latex whiskers implanted, and got a pair of green contact lenses. He even had surgery to give his lips a permanent snarl. Now all he needs is one last thing to make himself *purr*-fect: a fur graft on his body.

Checkmate

Matt Gone was self-conscious about how he looked without a shirt because of birth defects that left him missing muscles in his upper left chest and arm. The solution? He spent almost 20 years and more than $40,000 to help conceal them by covering his body with tattoos.

Face Time

Elaine Davidson, who lives in Edinburgh, Scotland, holds the world's record for the most body piercings—as of November 2003, she had 1,903 piercings!

Easy to Spot

Retired military man Tom Leppard (yes, that's his real name) is the most tattooed man in the world. The only parts of his body that have not been tattooed are the insides of his ears and the skin between his toes. He first got the idea for his total makeover when he spied a poster of a leopard in a London shop window. It was love at first sight. One year and $7,000 later, his new look was complete.

When Leppard retired after 28 years in the armed forces, he'd had enough of rules and regulations to last a lifetime. So after checking out various places on a map, he chose the remote Isle of Skye in Scotland as his new home. He built himself a hut and began his new life as a hermit. There are few people on the island to bother him, and Leppard's home is not easy to spot. It blends in so well with its surroundings that only those who know its location can find it.

Though he has no phone or modern conveniences, Leppard says he has all he needs: candlelight to read by, an extensive first-aid kit, and a whistle to use in case of an emergency. The nearby river is so clean and pure that he drinks its water and bathes in it every day. When Leppard runs out of food, he takes his kayak to the nearest village and stocks up. This is one leopard who is not likely to change his spots any time soon. His life is exactly the way he likes it.

EXTRA! EXTRA!

Oh, Rats!

From the late 1800s to the early 1900s, a man named Jack Black was, by appointment of Her Majesty Queen Victoria, the Royal Rat Catcher.

It's a Dog's Life

Dogs working as extras in Hollywood films in the 1930s received $7.50 a day—the same salary as people!

Petal Pushers

On Malaita, one of the Solomon Islands in the western Pacific Ocean, the Lau people once wore flowers in their ears and strung them through a hole in the end of their nose.

Bad Example

One elected official in ancient Sparta had an unusual job. He was paid to get drunk and stagger through the streets as a lesson to others in how not to behave!

Will Work for Food

It took 100,000 men about 20 years to build the Great Pyramid of Egypt. The workers were paid a healthy salary—of garlic, radishes, and onions.

Deep-Sea Die-ving

Deep-sea diving from oil rigs is the world's most dangerous job, with an annual death rate of one out of 100 divers. So why do they do it? They can make a lot of money in a short time—and, with luck, get out while they're still alive.

Hit Man

In 1999, Jun Sato of Tokyo, Japan, was having trouble finding a job. Then a TV show inspired him to try working as a human punching bag. Wearing a face mask and body padding, Sato charges people 1,000 yen (about $10) apiece to pummel him for up to three minutes at a time.

Wing Shift

Supermarket checkout woman Lynne Siddiq has never missed a day of work or even been late— which is all the more remarkable because she commutes from her home in Marbella, Spain, to her job in Blackburn, England. That's a total of 3,354 miles every week just to work three weekend shifts. Why does Siddiq do it? So she can stay in touch with her friends in England.

6

TAKE A BOW

CRAZY CONTESTS

 **Bug Bowl**

In August 2003, the annual Bug Bowl was held at Rutgers University in New Brunswick, New Jersey. To add to the festivities, its sponsors invented a new game called cricket spitting (left). Contestants spit brown house crickets, which are roughly the size of watermelon seeds, as far as they could. First prize went to Chris O'Donovan, who spit his cricket 28 feet 5.75 inches. A squirmy time was had by all!

What a Mug!

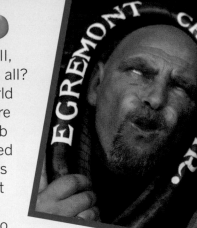

Mirror, mirror on the wall, who is the ugliest of them all? Each September, the World Gurning Championships are held at the Egremont Crab Fair in England's renowned Lake District. Competitors wearing horse collars test their skill at gurning—or twisting their features into ugly faces only a mother could love.

The winner receives a cash prize equaling about $200. The fair was first held in 1266, and one theory has it that the gurning contest got its start from the faces people made when they bit into the sour crabapples grown in the area.

NAKED GREED

Each day from February 29 to March 18, 2000, a clothing store in Vienna, Austria, offered $385 worth of merchandise to the first five customers daring enough to enter the store completely naked!

RIPLEY FILE: 11.12.31

Two-faced! Aileene Aalbu won a beauty pageant and a funny face contest—both on the same day.

Over the Hump

Watching the camel races in Virginia City, Nevada, is a lot different from watching horse races. Camels can be contrary, tossing riders at will or turning and running in the wrong direction. The winner of a camel race is not always the fastest camel, but the one that is best behaved!

ODDBALL SPORTS

Up on the Housetops

In free running, an extreme sport invented by Sebastien Foucan, participants scale buildings, run along narrow ledges, and jump from rooftop to rooftop. A TV documentary about Foucan and his team was filmed in London, England, where a series of photos (below) captured Foucan leaping from the bridge to the gun turret of the HMS *Belfast*. The team also used such landmarks as the Globe Theatre and the Royal Albert Hall as springboards for their leaps.

Frozen Fairways

The golf course greens are white in Uummannaq, Greenland, which is more than 360 miles north of the Arctic Circle. The wind chill can reach 58 degrees below zero—which doesn't keep top amateur golfers away from the World Ice Golf Championship tournament, held every March.

POOR SPORTS

When Romania lost its chance at the 2004 European soccer championships on a technicality, several frustrated fans hurled their TV sets out their windows.

It's a Snap!

Mark Davies of Darwin, Australia, has a peculiar method of motivating the 13- to 21-year-old members of his swim team to break their own records. He drops a crocodile into the pool. Since Davies started this practice, the swimmers' times have improved considerably.

Hard-Pressed

Invented in 1997 by Phil Shaw, extreme ironing takes ironing to new heights—and depths—in fact, anywhere from 331 feet under the ocean off the coast of Egypt to almost 21,000 feet high on a mountain in Argentina. Stunts were tamer but a whole lot sillier at the first Extreme Ironing Championship in Munich, Germany, in 2000. Competitors ironed while standing in a river, riding a bicycle, hanging upside down from a rock wall, jumping on a trampoline, kayaking, and much more.

RIPLEY FILE:
5.24.59

Horsing around! Jonathan James Toogood, a 19th-century equestrian from Overblow, England, astounded spectators by jumping hedges while riding backward.

PUSHING THE LIMITS

Bent Out of Shape

While in Japan on a Fulbright scholarship, Jonathan Nosan (right) of New York City decided to change from academics to acrobatics when he saw a contortionist perform in Tokyo. With no prior training, four years in circus schools enabled Nosan to bend, stretch, and balance his body in ways that most people wouldn't even think of trying. Nosan's company, ACROBACK, tours internationally, and his work has been featured in print, on TV, and in feature films—including acting as Jim Carrey's stunt double in *The Grinch*.

Pulling a Fast One

Kevin Fast (above) of Cobourg, Canada, has pulled off some really amazing feats of strength. After dragging two fire trucks at the same time for about 50 feet, Fast set a world record for pulling the heaviest truck for 100 feet. Then on June 7, 2003, he broke his own record when he pulled a 55,512-pound tractor trailer for 100 feet in a little over 48 seconds!

OUCH!

José Fernandez of Richmond, Virginia, could swallow razor blades and drive a nail up to the hilt into his head!

What a Hair-Raiser!

Joseph L. Greenstein (above) was 5 feet 4.5 inches tall and weighed 145 pounds, but he was a lot stronger than he looked. Known as "The Mighty Atom," Greenstein could bite a nail in half, lift a 470-pound weight with his teeth, and bend an iron bar with the resistance of his hair. In fact, his hair was so strong that in 1928, it was attached by a rope to an airplane—which Greenstein then kept from moving even though it was revving at 60 miles per hour!

A Real Eye Opener

Mahammed Sabir Sipra of Pakistan is a weight lifter—with a twist. Instead of lifting with his arms, Sipra uses his eyelids to lift up to 3.1 pounds. He's even better at lifting weights with his teeth—hefting as much as 68.2 pounds.

Flying High

On May 29, 1998, David "Cannonball" Smith was shot out of a cannon at a speed of 70 miles per hour! Smith picked himself up 185 feet 10 inches away, dusted himself off, and waved to his fans. In spite of the fact that he has been doing his circus act for 30 years, Smith still gets a bang out of his work.

RIPLEY FILE: 4.27.69

Long jump! King Teutobod, who ruled the Teutons from 125 to 101 B.C.E., could vault over the backs of six horses.

WHAT A STUNT!

Head Trip

Erik Sprague (right) loves reptiles. That's why he had himself made over to look like a lizard—complete with head-to-toe tattoos, a forked tongue, and a bony ridge implanted in his forehead. Sprague also maintains a very close relationship with his pet snake, Cricket, whom he's trained to slip up his nostril, slither down his throat, and exit through his mouth.

Upchuck Champ

Stevie Starr (left) has an unusual ability. He can swallow things and cough them up again, a talent that he picked up in a Glasgow orphanage and has since fine-tuned to a tee. Onstage, Starr, also known as "The Regurgitator," eats a bowl of sugar, drinks two glasses of water, and within seconds, brings the sugar up again—totally dry! Perhaps most perplexing of all is the stunt in which he swallows, in random order, seven glass eyeballs with letters printed on them. He coughs seven times and up they come, all in the right order. What do they spell? Ripley's, of course!

A Flying Leap

Rather than parachute from airplanes, BASE jumpers leap off fixed structures, such as buildings, bridges, and cliffs, which are usually less than 1,000 feet high. Once airborne, the jumpers free-fall, often deploying their parachutes only 10 to 15 seconds from the ground. In January 2004, 53 BASE jumpers leaped from the top of Kuala Lumpur's Petronas Twin Towers—the second tallest building in the world—during the Malaysian International Championship of Extreme Skydive/World Base Cup.

WELL BALANCED!

In the 1950s, world traveler Heinz Rox-Schulz paid for his trips by performing handstands on two bottles balanced one on top of the other on his suitcase.

RIPLEY FILE: 6.8.58

Shell game! Holder of the world jumping championship from 1882 to 1892, Joseph Darby (1862–1937) of Dudley, England, could jump from a standing position on and off an open basket of eggs with such lightning speed that he never cracked a single shell.

FABULOUS FEATS

Leap of Faith

The Land Divers of Pentecost, one of the islands of Vanuatu in the South Pacific, have been bungee-jumping for hundreds of years—but they use vines instead of bungee cords. The divers jump headfirst from an 80-foot-high tower. The vines attached to their ankles slow their plunges, but each year, some divers are injured when the vines snap. Why do they do it? It's a coming-of-age ritual, with boys as young as eight years old making their first jump.

King Bee

Apiculturist (bee expert) Dr. Norman Gary (left) is very comfortable around bees— even though he's been stung more than 75,000 times! Bees communicate with each other through liquid secretions called pheromones. To see what would happen, Gary smeared his body with the stuff. Within seconds, 60,000 bees were crawling all over him while he serenaded them with his clarinet! Next, upping the ante, Gary dripped artificial nectar onto his tongue and 109 bees flew into his mouth. Fighting the natural urge to gag, he kept his tongue still. One wrong move could have sent the bees into a stinging frenzy!

HIGH ON HERSELF

In 1931, Birdie Tillman swung across a tightrope stretched high above Times Square in New York City while hanging by her mouth from a metal bar attached to the rope.

Wingin' It

In 1984, stuntman Jim Tyler jumped out of a biplane over the Arizona desert and remained in free fall for more than one mile before landing on the back of the same plane!

RIPLEY FILE: 12.9.56

Showing his metal! Iron Man Sultan Beybars of Egypt (1223–1277) swam across the Nile River and back every day for 17 years—while clad in full armor and dragging a 38-pound weight.

Skywalker

Imagine walking a tightrope 30 stories above a city without a net. Now imagine doing that blindfolded! That's exactly what Jay Cochrane (below) did on November 11, 1998. Blindfolded, he crossed a tightrope stretched 600 feet between the two towers of the Flamingo Hilton Hotel in Las Vegas, Nevada.

Flamingo

EXTRA! EXTRA!

Strong-Armed!

On December 28, 1949, gymnast Glenn Sundby became the first person ever to walk down the 898 steps of the Washington Monument—on his hands.

Bagman

Terry Lyons holds the record for the most wins in an unusual race—the World Coal Carrying Championship held every Easter Monday in Gawthorpe, England. In the men's event, each contestant carries a 110-pound sack of coal as fast as he can from the Royal Oak public house to the maypole, a distance of 1,108.25 yards. Lyons won the championship eight times between 1977 and 1985.

Dying to Win

Every year, about a week before Halloween, Manitou Springs, Colorado, is host to the Emma Crawford Coffin Race. Each team of five brings its own coffin, mounted on wheels. One person plays Emma and rides in the coffin while four "mourners" push it down a hilly street. Prizes are awarded for the fastest coffin, the most creative coffin, and the "Best Emma."

Jawbreaker

Mighty-jawed Jackie Del Rio of Chicago, Illinois, could lift two tables and six chairs using only his teeth.

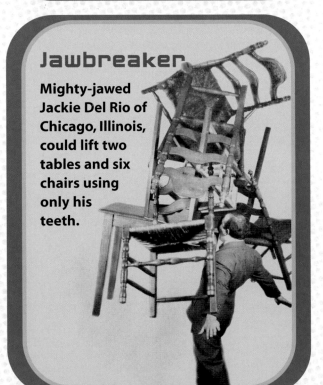

All Tied-Up

Melba Mueller of Texas could "tie" her arms behind her back at will.

Heavy Hitter

Joseph Ponder of Love Valley, North Carolina, could smash cement blocks with a 2-pound sledgehammer moving at 66 miles per hour—which he held with his teeth.

Hoop-Dee-Doo!

On September 18, 2000, Ken Kovach jumped through a hula hoop 129 times while somersaulting on a trampoline, breaking his previous world record of 122 jumps.

Taking a Dive

The La Quebrada cliffs in Acapulco, Mexico, are famous for cliff-diving, but no one has defied death as often as Raul Garcia, who has dived from the 87-foot-high cliffs 37,348 times!

Bull Session

Over 3,500 years ago, young women on the island of Crete practiced the sport of bull jumping—grabbing a charging bull by the horns and allowing the enraged animal to toss them onto its back.

Woolgathering

In September 2002, a sheep-counting contest was held for the first time in Hay, Australia. The fun began when about 400 sheep were let loose and made a mad dash past about 100 contestants, who tried to count them. The person who got closest to the real number won.

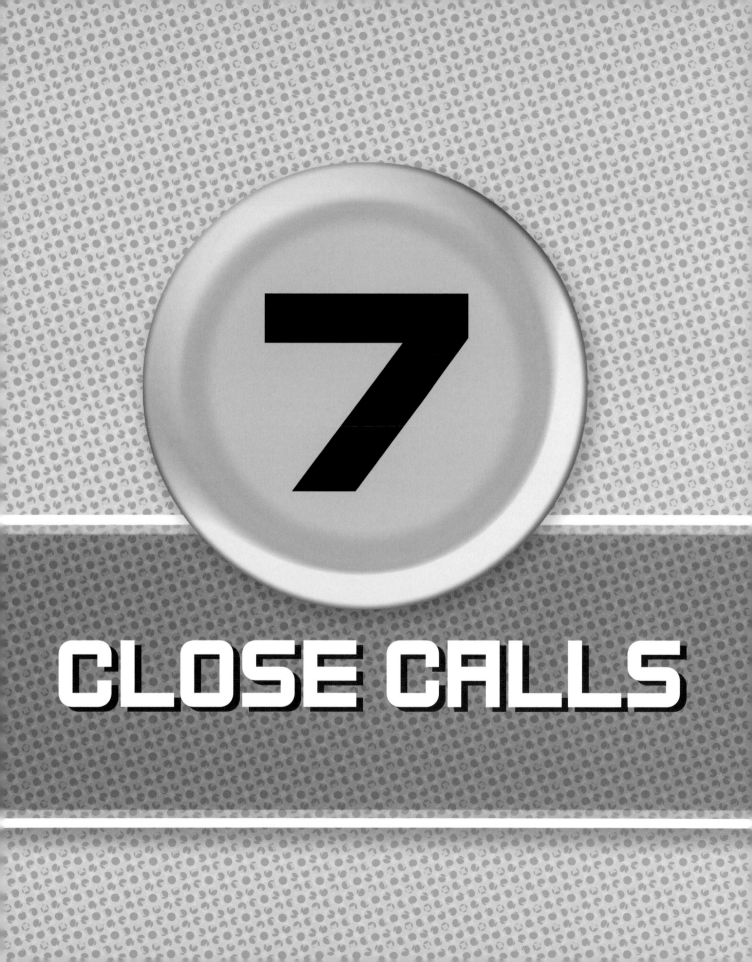

7

CLOSE CALLS

TAKING THE FALL

Plunging In

On October 20, 2003, 40-year-old Kirk Jones became the 14th person to take the plunge over Niagara Falls since 1901—and the first to survive wearing only the clothes on his back. Jones jumped into the Niagara River and glided over the 177-foot-high falls to the rocks below, smiling as he passed spectators. Jones walked away unharmed, probably because his fall was cushioned by compressed air forced under the water by the falls. Jones has since become the newest member of the Toby Tyler Circus in Texas.

Bailed Out

When a 32-year-old Austrian daredevil jumped from a 480-foot-high skyscraper in Berlin, Germany, in 2003, his parachute failed to open fully. Luckily, it got caught on a nearby crane, which saved him from crashing to the pavement but left him dangling 150 feet in the air. It took a rescue crew an hour to free him. Later, he was freed again—on bail, after being charged with making an illegal parachute jump.

NICE CATCH!

In 2001, nine-year-old Stephanie Boddy and six-year-old Samantha Quinn of Canada grabbed a picnic cloth and used it to catch and save a four-year-old boy who'd fallen out a fourth-floor window.

Fall Guy

The crowd was pumped. High in the air above them, Mike McGee and Greg Jones (below right) were about to try out a sport they'd invented themselves—para-bungee jumping, a thrilling combination of skydiving and bungee jumping. Tim McMahen would jump with them to record the stunt on videotape.

The men jumped out of the plane. When McGee reached 120 miles per hour—the maximum speed at which a human body can free-fall—he deployed his parachute. Jones was below, attached to McGee by a long bungee cord. The idea was that Jones would spring up on the cord once McGee's parachute opened. Instead, the speed of the fall caused the bungee cord to snap, striking Jones in the head like a giant, out-of-control slingshot and knocking him out. Unable to deploy his parachute, Jones began dropping like a rock.

McMahen collapsed his parachute to try and catch up to Jones. As the cameraman spiraled toward him, Jones regained consciousness long enough to deploy his chute. McMahen caught up, just as Jones was about to pass out again. McMahen then guided both their parachutes to the ground.

Within minutes of landing, Jones was airlifted to the nearest hospital. Any later and he would have died from his injuries. After a year and half of intense physical therapy, Jones was back up on his feet—but he gave up skydiving for good.

OOPS!

Loose Cannon

A 1981 concert had a most unintended result. It was staged by pacifist composer Luciano Berio (1925–2003), who arranged for a cannon to be fired as a protest against the destructiveness of war. Unfortunately, the resulting explosion injured several people and caused a fight to break out in the audience.

In the Toilet

When Edwin Gallart dropped his cell phone down a toilet in October 2003, he wasn't the only one who was sorry. The evening commuters on his train and thousands more on the trains behind were held up for hours. Why? When Gallart tried to retrieve the phone, he managed to get his arm stuck. It took rescue workers hours to free him because they had to take apart the entire toilet—and he still lost the cell phone.

MAJOR MISHAP

When drum major Steve Harding of Ventura, California, threw his baton into the air, it got tangled in two 4,000-volt power lines, which blacked out ten blocks, knocked out a radio station, and started a fire.

RIPLEY FILE:
4.5.59

Mis-guided! In the 1930s, Balthasar Nussbaumer of Austria was guiding a party of mountain climbers up the 12,054-foot-high Mount Grossvenediger. Suddenly his rope snapped, and he hurtled 1,000 feet down the mountain. Luckily, he walked away unharmed.

Fresh Fish

In 2001, chef Darren Smith was driving to his restaurant in Cornwall, England, when he had to slam on the brakes. On the seat next to him was a dead 7-foot-long shark that he was planning to cook that night. Though he avoided a collision, Smith instinctively used his free arm to brace himself against the seat—and stuck his hand right inside the shark's mouth, severing an artery and almost ripping off his thumb. Seventeen stitches later, Smith sheepishly told his doctor, "I must be the first person in history to be attacked by a shark on dry land—and a dead one at that!"

OUCH!

Such a Headache!

In August 2003, construction worker Ron Hunt (right) of Truckee, California, fell off his ladder and landed face-first on the drill he'd been using. Horrified, Hunt could feel the 18-inch-long, 1.5-inch-diameter drill bit go through his eye and out the back of his skull. Although doctors were unable to save his eye, Hunt is not complaining. Instead of piercing his brain, the drill bit pushed it aside. Had it not, Hunt probably wouldn't be around to talk about it!

A Cut Above

In April 2003, experienced outdoorsman Aron Ralston was hiking alone in a remote part of Utah when he found himself in a tight spot. He was climbing down from one ledge to the next in a narrow canyon when an 800-pound boulder shifted onto his right arm, pinning him in place. Ralston chipped away at the boulder, then tried using ropes and anchors to lift it, but nothing worked. Five days later, out of food and water, Ralston broke the bones near his wrist and used a pocketknife to amputate his lower arm and hand. He then rappelled, one-armed, 60 feet to the bottom of the canyon and walked six miles before a helicopter spotted him and airlifted him to the hospital. Within five months of his accident, Ralston had already hiked several 14,000-foot peaks and competed in a race that includes kayaking, running, and bicycle riding.

JUST SPIT IT OUT!

In 1990, 14-year-old Kevin Panten of Slinger, Wisconsin, was accidentally shot by a deer hunter. The bullet pierced his esophagus and shattered his jaw—but Panten spit it out and survived!

Hit and Run

In March 2000, 62-year-old Darlene Jones was on her way to the grocery store in Darby, Pennsylvania, when someone stabbed her in the back of the neck. Stunned, Jones stopped and turned, but her attacker was already gone. Thinking she'd only been punched, Jones continued on to do her shopping. Amazingly, no one noticed the steak knife sticking out of her neck—not even the cashier at the store! When Jones got home, her daughter saw the knife and pulled it out. After four days in the hospital and three months in rehab, Jones made a full recovery. The knife had missed her spinal cord by a mere one-half inch.

RIPLEY FILE: 9.6.59

Cushy landing! **When a cyclone blew through Massac County, Illinois, in 1860, Eliza State was swept through the air as she slept in her bed. She landed, unharmed, eight miles away in Pope County.**

On Guard!

A fisherman from the province of Kein Giang, Vietnam, survived being stabbed by a swordfish. The two-foot-long sword entered through his forehead and came out through his neck.

SAVED BY A WHISKER

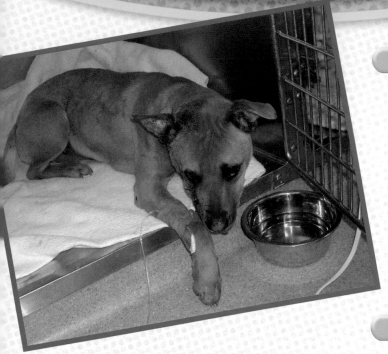

Frozen but Not Stiff

In April 2003, a dog named Dosha (left) was hit by a car in Clearlake, California. The police officer at the scene then shot her in the head to put her out of her misery and took her to an animal control center, where her body was placed in a freezer. A couple of hours later, the director of the center went to get Dosha's body—and found the dog standing up. Except for losing some of her hearing, Dosha made a full recovery!

For Deer Life

Gene Chaffin of Encinitas, California, rescued a pregnant doe after she had been struck by a car. He then delivered her two fawns by Caesarian section and saved one of them by performing mouth-to-mouth resuscitation.

Heartwarming

When their washing machine caught fire, everyone in the Newbold family was evacuated from their house in Nottingham, England—except Pikachu the hamster. When it was safe to go back inside, six-year-old Aran found Pikachu passed out on the floor. Luckily, a firefighter came to the rescue. He revived Pikachu with an oxygen mask and used his finger to give him chest compressions.

SNOWBALL'S CHANCE

Grover, a cat owned by the Futino family of St. Catherine, Canada, survived after spending a week buried under a 66-foot-high snow bank!

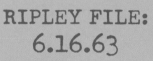

RIPLEY FILE: 6.16.63

Long haul! While pulling a sled full of freshly cut wood, Joseph Linsinger's horse suddenly collapsed in the snow. Without missing a beat, Linsinger, who lived in Eschenau, Austria, loaded the horse onto the sled and pulled it himself for 22 miles.

Alive and Kicking

When her small black dog, Sweetie (above), was hit by a mail truck in May 2001, Glenda Stevens was heartbroken. Stevens listened carefully for a heartbeat, and when she didn't hear one, she dug a grave in her backyard and tearfully buried her beloved pet. Hours later, Stevens saw Sweetie's hind legs sticking out of the ground. It seems that Sweetie wasn't dead after all, and was digging herself out! She'd suffered some broken bones, but a vet took care of them and Sweetie was back on her feet in no time.

EXTRA! EXTRA!

What a Drag!

In October 1991, Joe Petrowski of Manitoba, Canada, was in his backyard adjusting the sights on his rifle. He left the loaded gun for a few minutes—which was all it took for his dog Vegas to get her fur caught in the trigger. The gun went off and struck Petrowski in the back. The dog then dragged her wounded owner into the house, close to the phone so he could call for help.

A Hard-Knock Life

Lulu, a Chihuahua mix, was about to be put to sleep at a pound in Alabama when she was saved just in the nick of time by Nan LaSalle from an organization called Small Dog Rescue. You'd think one close call would be enough, but as LaSalle was driving Lulu home at 70 miles per hour along I-285, the dog jumped out of the open car window. Traffic swerved to avoid hitting Lulu as she rolled across the freeway, then got up and ran. Lulu was lucky this time, too. LaSalle stopped and gave chase. When she caught up with Lulu, all the dog had to show for her adventure were a few cuts and bruises!

Bad Slip-Up

In 1911, Bobby Leech survived going over Niagara Falls in a wooden barrel only to die several months later after slipping on a banana peel.

Chain Reaction

In 1966, Victor Surpitski of Ipswich, Massachusetts, survived a 60-foot fall from a cherry picker—while holding a running chain saw.

Card Trick

When their plane went down in 1991, four men spent two days drifting 100 miles in the Florida Gulf Stream with only three lifejackets among them. They were finally saved when they were able to signal a rescue plane by using their credit cards to reflect flashes of sunlight.

Double Trouble

Two-year-old Racine Gomez of Denver, Colorado, survived without injury, first when she fell from a three-story apartment window and second, when she was in her mother's car when it was hit by a tornado and rolled over three times.

Frozen Food

Before being spotted by fishermen, Henrik Carlsen, a Danish fisherman, survived 15 days in 1992 on an Arctic island off Greenland by lying under his boat and eating snow.

Stuck Up

When 14-year-old Duane Della of Altoona, Pennsylvania, tried to keep his two-year-old niece from climbing into the basement freezer, he lost his balance and toppled in, landing face-first. Duane opened his mouth to yell for help—and his tongue instantly stuck fast to the bottom of the freezer. Fortunately, firefighters were able to free his tongue and pull him out.

Free Fall

Carol Murray of Ontario, Canada, survived and is walking again after her parachute failed to open during her first skydive in 1997. She plunged 3,200 feet, landing on rain-softened ground.

8

CREEPY!

FREAKY!

Resting Assured

Writer Hans Christian Andersen (1805–1875) was so afraid of being mistaken for dead and buried alive that he kept a note on a bedside table that read, "I only seem dead."

RIPLEY FILE: 4.20.58

Double take! **In the Gardens of Maius in Rome, Italy, a giant 120-foot-high portrait of the Roman emperor Nero was destroyed by lightning on the very day in 68 C.E. that Nero took his own life in a villa four miles away.**

Standing Room Only

In 2003, Mayor Lütfü Efe came up with a unique solution to overcrowding in the cemetery in his village near Susurluk, Turkey: Dig up the dead and rebury them standing up. The village council didn't agree with the plan, but Efe is determined—and he practices what he preaches. Efe has added a clause to his will specifying that after his death, he be buried standing up.

The Earl of Antrim, Ireland, requested that he be buried upright on a hill so that he could look down on his castle, but drunken gravediggers buried him upside down by mistake!

Shiver Me Timbers!

A silver-plated skull thought to belong to Edward Teach, an 18th-century pirate known as Blackbeard, was exhibited beside his portrait in 1998 at the Mariner's Museum in Newport News, Virginia. Blackbeard was beheaded by British seamen during a battle off the North Carolina Coast in 1718. His head was placed on a stake at the mouth of the Hampton River as a warning to other pirates.

Custom Caskets

Kane Quaye Sowah of Accra, Ghana, creates coffins in unusual shapes, including giant lobsters, cocoa pods, cars, and chickens. Each coffin reflects the occupation of the deceased.

MUM'S THE WORD

Mummy or Daddy?

In June 2003, Joann Fletcher of the University of York, England, said that a mummy found in an Egyptian tomb in 1898 is Queen Nefertiti. The mummy resembles a famous bust of Nefertiti and has a shaved head—which Fletcher says the queen needed in order to wear her tight-fitting headpiece—and a double-pierced ear. However, archaeologist Zahi Hawass of Egypt says no female mummy has ever been found with a shaved head and that the mummy may actually be a teenage boy. As for the earrings, queens wore them in their wigs, not in their ears, and both men and women had pierced ears. The mummy remains silent on the subject.

Pet the Mummy

Cats, dogs, monkeys—even gazelles and crocodiles—were among the animals mummified by the ancient Egyptians. Some animal mummies were buried with their owners while others got their own coffins. A 3,500-year-old mummified monkey (right) is just one of the mummies that can be seen in the mummified pet section of the Egyptian Museum in Cairo.

HANDY TOOL

A mummified hand, cut from the body of a hanged man, was carried by burglars in ancient England who believed that it could open locked doors.

Freaky Forensics

The first thing you see when you enter the Forensic Museum in Bangkok, Thailand, is the museum's founder Khun Songkran Niyomsane. Well, not him exactly—just his skeleton. Continue on and you will see an assortment of body parts, bleeding brains, skulls with bullet holes, severed arms with tattoos, and a set of lungs with stab wounds.

The Forensic Museum attracts more visitors than any other museum or art gallery in Bangkok. They range from medical students and scientific researchers to homicide detectives and curiosity seekers. A case of skulls shot at from a variety of angles by forensic scientists shows just how bullets ricochet inside the brain— providing valuable information for police forensic teams to analyze as an aid to solving murder cases. In another room is a wall lined with glass display cases filled with jars of diseased organs—grim examples for medical students of what can go wrong with a human body.

However, the main attraction by far is the mummy of a serial killer from the 1950s whose shriveled body slumps against a glass enclosure that looks like a phone booth. Close inspection reveals an incision made when the brain was removed by scientists who wanted to find out if a criminal brain looked any different from a normal one. You may want to time your visit so that it's not too close to mealtime.

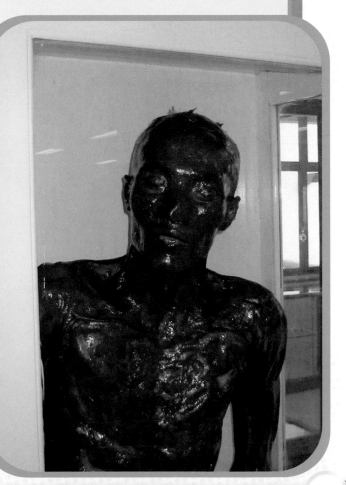

WAYS TO GO

Stiff Rules

When a family member dies, the Igorots of the Philippines stage a month-long banquet with the corpse propped in a chair as the guest of honor.

Sparkling Tribute

When 80-year-old Edna MacArthur of Alberta, Canada, died in 2002, her family wanted something besides photos to remember her by, so they had Grandma turned into a diamond and set in a gold ring! Fountain Garden Funeral Services is the first company to offer this service, which involves cremating the body and compressing it into a three-gram cube. The cube is flown to an Italian company that uses intense heat to convert it into carbon. It can then be crafted into a synthetic diamond. The cost? Just over $2,000—cheaper than a funeral and burial!

Severing Ties

Until recently, the Dani people (especially the women) of the Indonesian province of Irian Jaya cut off parts of their own body—usually a finger, but sometimes part of an ear—to mourn the death of a relative. The Dani people also used to smoke the bodies of certain village leaders until they were mummified (left). The mummies are still kept and are thought to have power and give protection to the villagers.

A TISKET, A CASKET

People of the Torres Strait Islands, near Australia, once placed the heads of corpses on anthills until they were picked clean, then painted them red and displayed them in baskets.

Drive-Through Funeral

If you weren't able to get to a wake on time at the G. W. Thompson Chapel of Remembrance in Spartanburg, South Carolina, it wasn't a problem. Between nine o'clock and midnight, you could zip through the drive-in lane, stop for a moment by the casket in the picture window, and pay your respects to the dead.

Good Spirits

The Uape people of the Upper Amazon in Brazil drink the ashes of their cremated dead mixed with casiri, a local alcoholic beverage, in the belief that they will absorb all the good qualities of the deceased.

RIPLEY FILE:
8.14.49

Funeral on ice! Enclosed by an arm of the River Spree, the Spreewald, just south of Berlin, Germany, is an area made up of waterways that feed into the river. The Wends people who live there once used them as roads. In winter, mourners in funeral processions would put on their ice skates and pull the casket, which was mounted on a sled, along the ice.

BOO!

In Good Spirits

The Phi Ta Khon festival that takes place every June in Dan Sai, Thailand, commemorates the return of Buddha in his next-to-last incarnation. The occasion was such a joyous one that even the village spirits took part in the welcoming parade. Today, village men dress up as the spirits, wearing colorful masks and costumes, and mingle good-naturedly with the crowd.

Flaming Passion

A wall near the main entrance to the Junagarh Fort in Bikaner, India, is covered with the handprints of Hindu women—each of whom followed her husband in death by throwing herself on his funeral pyre.

WORTH THEIR SALT

It is a custom in Japan for the family of a deceased person to hand out small packets of salt to mourners, since salt is believed to protect them from the ghosts of the dead.

Spook Spray

Mary Elizabeth Feldman of Charleston, South Carolina, invented Aunt Mary's Ghost Away, a chamomile-based spray that children can use against ghosts and monsters they believe live under the bed.

Polter-Guests

In Holland House in London, England, the poet Percy Bysshe Shelley (1792–1822) reported meeting an apparition of himself—and died soon afterward.

RIPLEY FILE: 11.69.61

Scared to death! King George I (1660–1727) of England divorced his wife, Sophia Dorothea (1666–1726), in 1694 and kept her imprisoned for 32 years—until her death. On June 11, 1727, a note was tossed into his coach. It was from Sophia and said that the king would be summoned to divine judgement within a year after her death. The frightened king died on the spot.

EXTRA! EXTRA!

Head Case

When England's Sir Walter Raleigh was beheaded in 1618, his wife, Elizabeth, buried his body but kept his embalmed head in a bag for the last 29 years of her life. It then passed to their son Carew. When Carew died in 1666, Sir Walter's head was buried with him.

Cushy Nests

The ancient Egyptians mummified falcons, which represented the god Horus, son of Osiris and Isis, and buried them in elaborate tombs along the Nile River.

Double Duty

Down to Earth Coffins in Chichester, New Hampshire, builds custom-made caskets that can be used as bookcases, tables, or even gun cabinets until they are needed for burial.

Uh-Oh!

Dutch hearse driver Lucien Van Wijngaarden of Amsterdam, the Netherlands, is out of a job. Why? Because in August 2003, he lost a coffin on his way to a funeral! Wijngaarden failed to notice when the back doors of the hearse flew open. It was not until he arrived at the cemetery empty-handed that he realized something was missing!

Grand Send-Off

Concert pianist Madge Ward's gravestone is a 25-ton black granite grand piano.

Surprise!

Old Man's Day is celebrated on October 2 in Hertfordshire, England, to commemorate the survival of Matthew Wall, a 16th-century farmer, who was revived when the pallbearers slipped on some leaves and dropped his coffin onto the road. Wall lived to a ripe old age.

Headliner

On March 6, 1978, the Royal Swedish Academy of Sciences bought the skull of Emanuel Swedenborg (1688–1772), which had been stolen from his casket in the 1850s, at auction for $10,560. The skull was then returned to his sarcophagus in Uppsala, Sweden. Swedenborg, a philosopher and theologian, was said to have abnormal psychic powers. He published more than 50 books.

What a Fun-eral!

To help provide a sense of the deceased's personality, the Batesville Casket Company advises funeral directors on how to create theme funerals. For instance, if the deceased was a big sports fan, the funeral parlor could be set up like a rec room, complete with a big-screen TV, a recliner, and lots of sports paraphernalia. The TV remote and a box of popcorn can be tucked into a drawer in the casket for otherworldly viewing.

Major Role Reversal

An ambulance in Nykroppa, Sweden, was sent out to pick up Lars Elam, a patient with a high fever. The ambulance returned to the hospital with Elam behind the wheel, and the regular driver lying dead in the back from a heart attack.

Dying to Move In

Verna Richardson, designer and president of Habco, Inc., a company in Madison, Wisconsin, makes caskets that look like 6-foot-long houses.

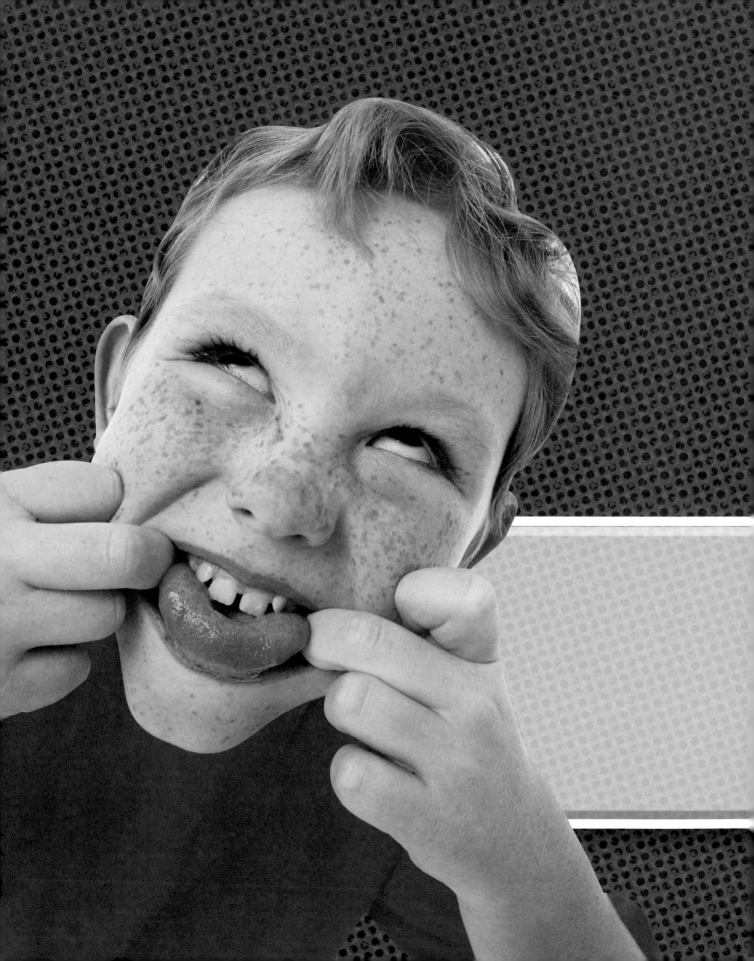

9

BODY MATTERS

VERY FISHY!

How Re-volt-ing!

In ancient Rome, shock treatments were used to treat headaches and joint pain. These treatments were used long before electricity was invented. So how were the shocks delivered? By torpedo fish, or electric rays. To cure headaches, a live fish was placed against the patient's head, while joint pain was treated by having the patient stand on the fish in a pool of saltwater.

A Bundle of Nerves

Since 1972, Dartmouth College biology professor George Langford has been studying squid to learn about human memory and why certain diseases cause forgetfulness. Like humans, a squid's memory depends on nerves, which are carried by axons, making proper connections within its brain. Squid have much larger axons than humans, making it easier to observe how electrical connections are made. Langford hopes to find out which proteins are present or absent when the connections between nerves have been disrupted. If he succeeds, a cure for memory loss may not be far behind!

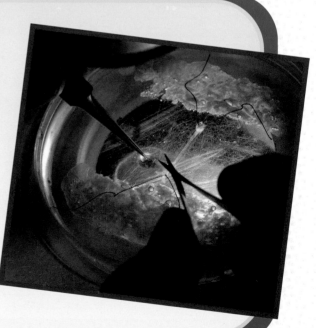

WEEDING THEM OUT

In 1991, doctors in American clinics and hospitals began using seaweed in dressings to treat skin ulcers.

Blue Bloods

The United States government is limiting the number of horseshoe crabs that can be used for bait. Why? There's something in these odd-looking creatures' blue-colored blood that scientists find very valuable. They use it to test for bacteria in medicines. Each year about 300,000 crabs are bled and then placed back into their natural habitats. The process is quick and painless, and the crabs are no worse for wear.

EYE-OPENERS

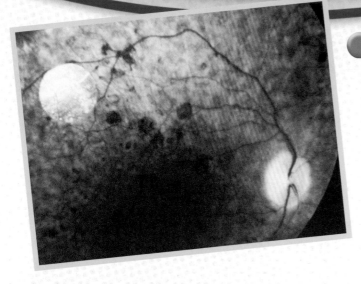

Eye-deal Treatment

Until very recently, people with diseased retinas had no hope of ever seeing again. Now a company called Optobionics has invented an artificial retina. It's actually a silicon chip that converts light into electrical signals, which then travel through the optic nerve to the brain. Paul Ladis of Roselle, Illinois, who was legally blind for ten years, had one implanted in his eye in November 2002. Though Ladis's vision is not perfect, he is delighted with the result. Where he once saw only darkness, he can now see shapes, lights, and objects in motion!

Deep Seeing

For most of us, things look blurry underwater, but that's not the case in the Surin Islands of Thailand. Scientists at Sweden's Lund University have discovered that children of the Moken people, who live on boats or in stilt houses near the sea, have extremely good underwater vision. When underwater, most people's pupils expand to let in more light, but the Thai children's pupils get smaller. They work like pinhole cameras, which use tiny holes instead of lenses to focus light and make images. Have the children learned how to shrink their pupils or are they born with that ability? The scientists are still trying to find out.

SEEING IS BELIEVING

The retina of the human eye has 137 million cells—130 million for seeing black and white, and seven million more to see colors.

RIPLEY FILE: 9.21.58

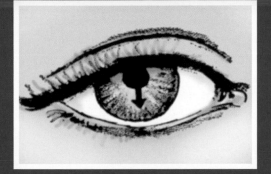

An eyeful! Shirley Santos of New Bedford, Massachusetts, has an arrowhead-shaped birthmark in the iris of her right eye and her twin brother has the identical marking in his left eye.

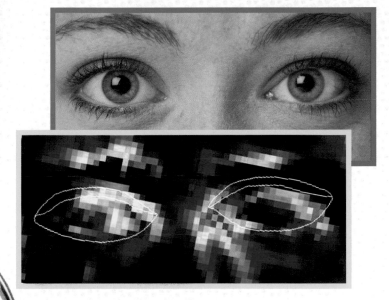

Splel Chcek

Resraechres at Cmabirgde Uinvrestiy fnuod taht the odrer ltteers are wtitren in deson't mttaer as lnog as the frist and lsat letrets are in the rgiht palce. Yuo'll be albe to raed the wrods croerclty no mtater how jubmled the lteters are. It semes taht yuor barin dosne't raed ecah leettr but sees the wohle wrod at ocne.

Eyewitness

Researchers in Minnesota have come up with a new kind of lie detector—a camera that records heat patterns as white areas on the skin. When a person tells a lie, the blood rushes to his or her face, increasing the temperature in that area. So when a test subject lies in front of the camera, a white ring appears around the eyes, immediately giving away the liar.

MEDICAL MYSTERIES

A Leap of the Imagination

In 1642, doctors were baffled by the bizarre case of Catharina Geisslerin of Germany. She claimed that she'd swallowed tadpoles while swimming and that there was a community of frogs thriving in her intestinal tract. To prove it, she vomited full-grown frogs on command! Finally, one doctor dissected a vomited frog and was amazed to find that its stomach was full of black flies. How did they get there if the frog had been living in Geisslerin's stomach? Geisslerin must have regularly swallowed full-grown frogs and vomited them up soon afterward.

Solar Power

Hira Ratan Manek of Kerala, India, is a man who hates to eat. He stopped eating solid food when he was age 53 and has been living on nothing but sunshine and liquids ever since! "He eats through his eyes," his wife explained, noting that he stares at the sun for an hour every day—a medical mystery in itself since staring at the sun can make you blind. Manek believes that humans use only 5 percent of their brain, and that they can tap the other 95 percent through the sun's energy. Hoping to gain insight into how to solve food storage problems on expeditions, NASA has been studying Manek's technique. So far they have verified that he has gone 130 days without food.

WHAT GALL!

In China, cow gallstones, which are used in traditional herbal medicines, sell for almost $4,000 a pound.

RIPLEY FILE: 2.16.77

Bloodless!
Dr. Charles Drew (1904–1950) of Washington, D.C., who pioneered discoveries in preserving blood plasma, bled to death after being injured in an automobile accident.

Visual Aid

Colonel J. Hunter Reinburg of Wabasso, Florida, was rejected as a midshipman because of his poor eyesight. He then came up with a do-it-yourself cure: piercing his ears and nose with paper clips. Apparently it worked, because Reinburg went on to have a distinguished flying career!

Wriggly Diet

A worm a day keeps the doctor away—at least that's what 39-year-old firefighter Paisit Chanta believes. It all started about 30 years ago when he was out fishing near his village in Thailand. He was really, really hungry and didn't have anything to eat but bait. He figured since fish don't die from eating worms, he'd try a few himself. Chanta's been eating the wriggly little creatures ever since. He says he is very healthy and credits his wormy diet with keeping him that way.

INSIDE SCOOP

Crunch!

In July 2003, an Israeli woman was cleaning her house when a cockroach flew into her mouth. To make matters worse, she ended up swallowing the fork she was using to try to pry it out of her throat. After an X-ray showed the fork was wedged sideways in her stomach, she had surgery to remove it. The cockroach, however, had already been digested.

HARD TO SWALLOW

In 1927, a 42-year-old woman was rushed to the hospital with stomach pains. X-rays showed 2,533 objects in her stomach, including 947 bent pins and other metal odds and ends.

Not Too Sharp

In 1993, Tyro, a three-month-old Labrador retriever puppy in British Columbia, Canada, made a full recovery after swallowing a nine-inch-long knife!

Hard to Stomach

In 1822, a Canadian named Alexis St. Martin (1794–1880) was accidentally shot in the stomach. When St. Martin's stomach healed, there was still a gaping hole in his side. The doctor who treated him, William Beaumont (1785–1853), made the best of the botched surgery by using the six-inch hole to discover the secrets of digestion.

Beaumont became the first person to observe human digestion while it was happening. He tied a silk string to different kinds of foods and dangled the morsels through the hole into St. Martin's stomach. Cooked beef, raw beef, boiled chicken, stale bread, and raw cabbage are just some of the foods the doctor experimented with. After inserting the food, he would send St. Martin back to whatever he had been doing. Later, at varying intervals, Beaumont would pull out the food. Beaumont discovered that chicken was digested more slowly than beef, that

vegetables took the longest to digest, and that milk curdled before it could be digested.

In another experiment, Beaumont put some of St. Martin's stomach juices in a vial to see if food digested faster outside the stomach. He found that the food in the vial was not digested at all because it was cold, and the digestive process requires a certain amount of heat to work. Beaumont became famous for discovering that hydrochloric acid is part of the human digestive process.

Poor St. Martin soon tired of being a human guinea pig. With each experiment, he became angrier. The good doctor made the best of this development as well, by observing that stress can hinder digestion!

THAT'S GROSS!

On File

If you never cut your fingernails, each one would grow to about 13 feet long by the time you reached the age of 80. Romesh Sharma (below) of India has been growing the nails of his left hand for 40 years. In 2003, their combined length totaled more than 32.8 feet—setting a new world record.

Wash It Out with Soap!

More germs live inside the human mouth than in any other part of the body. In fact, 100 million tiny organisms camp out in your mouth, eating the leftovers, pooping, mating, and having babies—all in an average day. That's more than all the people who lived in California, New York, Texas, Florida, and New Jersey in 2000 put together!

RIPLEY FILE: 3.21.98

Sucking up! In the early 1850s, a French doctor named François Broussais (1772–1838) treated his indigestion by applying 50 to 60 leeches to his body 15 times in 18 days.

LET THEM EAT DIRT

Children touch their mouths with their hands about once every three minutes and end up swallowing enough dirt each day to cover seven floor tiles.

Lousy Research

In the past, scientists who created lice shampoos found it hard to study head lice. That's because the creatures die as soon as they're plucked from heads. Lice are parasites that need the blood of other species to survive. So the researchers came up with the perfect solution. The lice live on membranes and hair dangling in human blood inside a test tube. The artificial scalp is the perfect environment to keep the pests alive just long enough to find out the best way to kill them!

Achoo!

Run for cover! Here's an amazingly gross though little-known fact: The drops of moisture in a sneeze can travel up to 150 feet per second. That's 102 miles per hour!

Eye Strain

Having trouble keeping your eyes open? That could be because your eyelids are heavy with hundreds of microscopic creatures called follicle mites—like the three white, wormy-looking things at the right—that live at the roots of your eyelashes.

EXTRA! EXTRA!

Double Vision

The pharaohs of ancient Egypt had personal physicians to treat individual parts of their body, including separate doctors for each eye.

Coinci-dental!

In 1991, while having dental surgery, Wendy McGarr, a deaf woman from Guelph, Canada, regained her ability to hear.

Leaping Lizards!

Two early treatments for skin diseases were to roll in the grass on the morning of Saint John's Day and to eat a lizard.

Speech Therapy

During the Middle Ages, a cure for stuttering was to apply hot irons and spices to patients' tongues.

Nose Sense!

The olfactory nerves found in the human nose are the only nerves in the entire human body that can regenerate themselves.

Say It Snot True

Mucus is made in the lining of the nose. When you have a cold, your nose gets runny because your body is trying to flush out those cold germs. Even when you're not sick, you swallow about a quart of nose mucus every single day.

Picture This!

The lenses in your eyes continue to grow throughout your entire life.

Hearsay

In 1992, dentist Barry Mersky of Bethesda, Maryland, invented a hearing aid that fits inside a tooth. Mersky based his invention on the principle that a person's teeth and skull are good conductors of sound. A tiny microphone hidden in a shirt or blouse pocket picks up sound and sends it to a dental retainer containing an antenna and amplifier. A crystal bonded to a tooth converts the sound to vibrations that travel through a person's head to his or her ear.

Knee-jerk Response

Connie Munro of Juneau, Alaska, underwent knee surgery but did not regain the full use of her leg until she was charged by a black bear and forced to run for her life.

Medical Marvel

In 1993, Dr. Anna Perkins, a 93-year-old physician in Westerloo, New York, still charged the same rates she had originally set in 1928—$4 for an office visit, $5 for a house call, and $25 to deliver a baby!

Virtual Vistas

The Stanford University Medical Center in California has rooms with digital window scenes of sunrises and sunsets that simulate the passage of time for recovering patients.

Twisted!

In the 19th century, patients suffering from a stiff neck wore a metallic collar equipped with thumbscrews.

Showing Her Metal

Sofie Herzog (1848–1925), a pioneer doctor in Texas, wore a necklace made of 24 bullets that she had removed from wounded gunfighters. Considering it her good-luck necklace, Herzog wore it often and was even buried with it.

10

ODDS AND ENDS

SQUIRRELLY!

Hubcap Queen

Lucy Pearson has been collecting hubcaps for more than 40 years. Each time a car came into her husband's wrecking yard in Pearsonville, California, she would pop off and save the hubcaps. Now she gets calls from car buffs all over the world who are looking for special models from a certain year. Pearson knows exactly where each and every one of her 200,000 hubcaps is and can put her hands on the one she needs within minutes!

A Lot of Fluff

In 1984, Graham Barker started digging lint out of his belly button each day before showering. To date, Barker has accumulated a bit more than two jars full. He's not sure how he will use it, but hopes that it might come in handy some day.

A Head Start

When it comes to weird collections, it would be hard to top Robert Ripley's set of shrunken heads! His specimens were obtained from the Jivaro people of Ecuador, who believed that to decapitate an enemy and possess his head was to keep for one's self all the attributes of its original owner.

Ghosty Men

Langley and Homer Collyer lived in a luxurious mansion on Fifth Avenue in New York City. When their once exclusive neighborhood began to go downhill, the brothers began to keep to themselves. At night, they scoured the neighborhood for discarded junk, which they piled in front of boarded-up windows and doorways to booby-trap anyone who might try to get in. As the years passed, the brothers accumulated so much junk they needed tunnels to get through it. Neighborhood children called them the "ghosty men" because of their long, white, matted hair and tattered appearance.

In the 1930s, Homer, paralyzed and blind, became dependent on Langley. Then on March 21, 1947, the police received a call that there was a dead body in the mansion. They went to investigate but couldn't get in the door. After breaking a second-floor window and tossing out piles of garbage to get through, they found Homer, dead after having not eaten for days. But what had become of Langley?

Sanitation workers started clearing out the junk. Out came chandeliers, old pianos, car parts, and thousands of newspapers. After removing 103 tons of junk, they finally found Langley. He had been buried alive while crawling through a tunnel to feed his brother—done in by the very junk he had put there to booby-trap intruders!

FLAKY FASHIONS

Skin Tight

With water-based paint and careful brush strokes, Filippo Ioco has created a new fashion in swimwear—the painted-on bathing suit! The swimwear is so authentic-looking that people don't realize his models are really wearing nothing at all! Swimmers beware—the paint is not waterproof!

Threads from Treads

The orders keep rolling in to Zuss Fashion Design, owned by sisters Krijnie and Christa de Leeuw Van Weenen of the Netherlands, who create clothes for both men and women. Oddly enough, the sisters find most of their materials in Dumpsters. That's because they fashion their clothes out of used rubber inner tubes from bicycle and moped tires. Using their own patterns, the sisters cut them up, then punch holes in them to weave or lace them together. Customers can visit their website, www.zuss.com, to choose from the featured hats, dresses, skirts, tops, pants, and vests.

SEEING RED

In Thailand, people who are born on Sunday traditionally wear the color red. Why? They believe it will bring them good fortune.

Living Jewels

In the Yucatán area of Mexico, people comb the forest for ma'kech beetles so they can make them into living jewelry. They apply nontoxic glue to the beetles' tough outer wings and affix decorative stones. Then they add a little gold ring and attach a chain leading to a brooch. The process is made easier because the beetles play dead when they feel threatened. With proper care, these living works of art can last for two years.

Locks-Smith

Hairdresser Bill Black of St. Louis, Missouri, has found a use for the hair clippings that land on his floor. He creates clothing. One of his human hair bikinis sold for $350.

RIPLEY FILE: 6.24.45

Once upon a time . . . Marie de' Medici (1573–1642), queen of France, was the owner of the most expensive dress of all time. It was adorned with 39,000 pearls and 3,000 diamonds. Although the gown cost the equivalent of $20,000,000, de' Medici wore it on September 14, 1606, for her daughter's christening—and never put it on again!

SPECIAL EFFECTS

It's a Wrap

A key element in the art of Christo and Jeanne-Claude is that it's temporary. Though their projects may take years to complete, none of them remain in place for more than a few weeks. Whether it's wrapping entire buildings, surrounding 11 islands in Florida with pink fabric, or wrapping 178 trees in Berower Park, Riehen, Switzerland, with translucent fabric, these artists use the whole world as a canvas for their art.

FANCY FOOTWORK

Artist Paul Warhola of Pittsburgh, Pennsylvania, brother of Andy Warhol, displayed an exhibit of paintings he created using chicken feet as brushes.

Beetlemania

Artist Jan Fabre was hired by the Queen of Belgium to redecorate the Hall of Mirrors in the Royal Palace in Brussels. To the queen's astonishment, Fabre used the shiny, iridescent wing cases of Asian jewel beetles to create a mural as well as to cover the main chandelier. Everyone who sees the hall agrees that the effect is quite dazzling and not creepy at all!

Blow by Blow

Dale Chihuly can do things with glass that no one's ever done before. Often, his amazing glass sculptures combine color and water, but he says, "It is really light that makes those materials come alive." Chihuly's 31-foot-tall Tower of Light (above), built for the Contemporary American Sculpture show in Monte Carlo, Monaco, combines all three—not to mention the wild, uninhibited forms that give his work real attitude.

ANIMAL MANIA

Dog Days

Is your dog stressed? If so, you might consider taking him or her to a Ruff Yoga class. A New York City gym is already offering yoga classes for humans and their dogs and is considering expanding it to its other branches. Students do all the traditional poses, but with a twist—their dogs are incorporated into the moves.

Stuffed Animals

Teenager Amy Ritchie of Midland, North Carolina, has an unusual job. It all started when she found a dead snake in her backyard and decided that it would make a fine belt. Since then she has taken up taxidermy—the art of preparing and stuffing the skins of dead animals. So far Ritchie has stuffed squirrels, mice, deer, and even a tiger cub. Now she's so good at it that she no longer needs to practice on highway roadkill supplied by her father—she's got her own business and is winning top prizes at taxidermy competitions.

Monkey Business

Each year in November, there is a magnificent banquet in the town of Lop Buri, Thailand. Yongyuth Kijtwattananuson, the proprietor of a local hotel, sets up tables with napkins and menus in the nearby temple ruins, a popular tourist site. He then lays out a delicious vegetarian feast for 600 guests—all of whom are monkeys!

Oh, Rats!

Each year, thousands of faithful Hindus journey to the state of Rajasthan, India, to visit the Karni Mata Temple and pay tribute to its sacred rats. The place is crawling with the rodents, which flock to large bowls of milk and food put out for them. Many people offer the rats food from their hands. It is said that the rats carry the souls of storytellers and, when they die, will come back as people.

NEW AND NUTTY!

Phone Home

In 2002, two British researchers created a model for a high-tech receiver that can be embedded in one of your own molars. The voice of anyone who calls would be turned into vibrations that travel through your skull to your inner ear, where only you can hear them. The catch? You can only listen—you can't talk back!

Over the Top!

With ingredients such as essential oils of basil and oregano combined with tomato extract, Experimenta of Duccio Cresci, an Italian cosmetics firm has created a new line of bath products that smell exactly like pizza!

Soft As a Feather

Scientists at the United States Department of Agriculture have developed a method of converting chicken feathers into disposable diapers!

BUBBLE TROUBLE

A Denver, Colorado, company called Excuse Me, Inc., makes a soda called Rudy Begonia's Belcher that promises to deliver explosively loud belches after drinking it.

What a Gas!

Researcher Buck Weimer of Pueblo, Colorado, spent several years performing experiments in an effort to develop a product that would filter out bad smells. He came up with Under-Ease, underwear with a charcoal filter that will remove stinky gases before they escape into the air. Under-Ease is available for both men and women—and the filter can be replaced when it wears out.

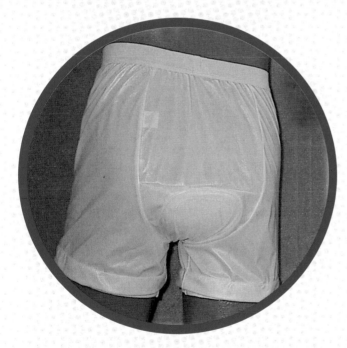

Sun Dial

SunWatch not only tells the time but also buzzes to warn wearers when they are in danger of getting a sunburn.

RIPLEY FILE:
4.26.2000

Snow job! John Sweeney of Darien, Connecticut, will get out his snowmaker and blanket a homeowner's lawn with real snowflakes for a fee of $1,000.

Don't Mess

A company in New York City makes a plastic and steel wallet that can only be opened with a four-digit code. If forced open, it will self-destruct.

HEAVEN SENT!

Getting the Poop

In June 2003, a horde of gypsy moth caterpillars descended on Oakland Park in Pontiac, Michigan. There were so many that visitors could actually hear them crunching leaves. Pedestrians were forced to carry umbrellas to protect themselves from the tiny poop pellets raining down from the trees.

Pop Go the Crickets

"You drive down the street and they pop like Bubble Wrap," said Amy Nisbet of Elko, Nevada. She was describing the invasion of Mormon crickets that appeared out of the blue in June 2003 and covered almost every square inch of her town. The highways got so slippery after thousands of the 2.5-inch-long insects were squashed by cars that electronic overhead signs had to be programmed to alert motorists to slow down.

RIPLEY FILE: 4.30.30

Rain of fire! The early morning skies over eastern North America were lit up on November 13, 1833, by 200,000 shooting stars! None of them reached Earth.

FLAKY!

Ribbet!

Hurricane Isabel not only brought the usual high winds and driving rain but also dropped something quite unexpected—frogs' eggs! Scientists think the hurricane, which hit the East Coast of the United States in September 2003, must have picked up the eggs in North Carolina and dropped them in Berlin, Connecticut. One resident, Primo D'Agata, kept a mass of them in a glass of water, waiting for them to sprout legs.

Waste Not, Want Not

The 10,000 tourists that descend on Sugarloaf Mountain Ski Resort every winter were too many for the town's sewage system to handle. The problem became so serious that only a drastic solution would do. Then someone had the bright idea of turning the sewage into snow. "How?" you might ask. First, the sewage travels through pipes to a facility where it is treated with chemicals to get rid of harmful bacteria. From there, it's piped to a plant where it's frozen and sent through snow machines.

EXTRA! EXTRA!

Lots of Luck

Norman Wayne Bright of Heber Springs holds an official license from the Arkansas Game and Fish Commission to hunt four-leaf clovers. To date, his collection numbers more than 7,000.

Brown Bagging It

Anton Schiavone of Bangor, Pennsylvania, used paper grocery bags to build a life-sized replica of *The Last Supper* by Leonardo Da Vinci.

Yuk!

People racing yachts in the 1976 Olympic Games in Montreal, Canada, were pelted by wriggling things falling from the sky during a storm. It didn't take them long to figure out that the rain was chock-full of live maggots!

Red Caps

On October 14, 1775, red snow fell over the Swiss Alps. The snow got its color from red algae that grows in Alpine regions.

Really Spacey

In March 2003, Dan Foley, a New Mexico state representative, introduced a bill to proclaim every second Thursday in February Extraterrestrial Culture Day. The day would "celebrate and honor all past, present, and future extraterrestrial visitors" to the state where UFO buffs believe an alien spacecraft crash-landed in 1947.

Scent-sation

Kanebo, a cosmetic company in Japan, has developed a line of pantyhose that are embedded with vitamins and special scents that are released when they come into contact with skin.

Over Easy

In northern Alaska's frigid temperatures, which can reach 60 degrees below zero, eggs will bounce like rubber balls if left outside too long.

Hot Stuff

Captain Maurice Seddon of Berkshire, England, invented a tracksuit, a dressing gown, and gloves heated by 12 volts of electricity.

Safety Briefs

In 1998, Katsuo Katugoru of Tokyo, Japan, whose greatest fear is drowning, designed underpants that would inflate 30 times their original size should he be caught in a tidal wave. Unfortunately, Katugoru accidentally set them off while riding on a crowded subway at rush hour. Fortunately, one passenger had the presence of mind to deflate the underpants by stabbing them with a pencil.

Quack, Quack!

In 1990, Nicholas Graham of San Francisco, California, invented Joe Boxer's Undo-Vision—underwear with 3-D images of fish, ducks, and Godzilla on them.

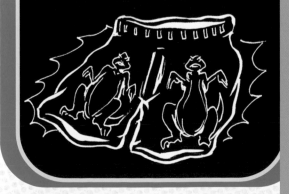

We'd Love to Believe You!

Do you have a Believe It or Not! story that has happened to you or to someone you know? If it's really weird and if you would like to share it, the people at Ripley's would love to hear about it. You can send your Believe It or Not! entries to:

The Director of the Archives
Ripley Entertainment Inc.
7576 Kingspointe Parkway, Suite 188
Orlando, Florida 32819

INDEX

PHOTO CREDITS

Ripley Entertainment Inc. and the editors of this book wish to thank the following photographers, agents, and other individuals for permission to use and reprint the following photographs in this book. Any photographs included in this book that are not acknowledged below are property of the Ripley Archives. Great effort has been made to obtain permission from the owners of all materials included in this book. Any errors that may have been made are unintentional and will gladly be corrected in future printings if notice is sent to Ripley Entertainment Inc., 7576 Kingspointe Parkway, Suite 188, Orlando, Florida 32819.

…EA FC

…NUAL 2016

…rd Godden, James Sugrue

…terson

…unications Ltd., Edinburgh, under licence from
…www.chelseafc.com. Printed in the EU.

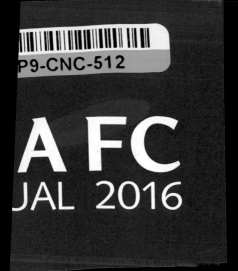

A FC

JAL 2016

...dden, James Sugrue

...ns Ltd., Edinburgh, under licence from
...elseafc.com. Printed in the EU.

...on; Action Images and Shutterstock.

4